MW00791113

My Life With 40 Parents

To Suzanne,
with love!

Christopher
Brooks :)

My Life With 40 Parents

INTIMATE REFLECTIONS
OF A FOSTER CHILD

CHRISTOPHER BROOKS

Copyright © 2018 Christopher Brooks

All rights reserved. No part of this book may be reproduced, stored in a
retrieval system, or transmitted in any form or by any means—electronic,
mechanical, photocopy, recording, scanning, or other—except for brief
quotations in critical reviews or articles, without the prior written
permission of the author.

This book is dedicated to my mother. The beautiful and loving lady that carried me inside her belly for nine months, so that I could have the opportunity to explore this beautiful planet. You weren't able to raise me, but you gave me an incredible gift, Life. And for that, I'll always be grateful.

To the Pierce's, Tony, Thom, Kathleen, Terry and all the other kind and beautiful souls who accepted me, loved me and guided me throughout this journey.

To Melissa for helping me find and reconnect with my family. And for supporting me in those moments when things got awkward and uncomfortable.

And to the sweet and beautiful Leticia. For having the courage to crawl through the thick thorn bushes around my heart. For showing me what unconditional love looks and feels like. And for continuously encouraging me to shine my light. You helped me heal and grow in more ways than I may ever be able to express.

Special Thanks
to

Terry Woods, Greg Muller, and Rosa Penn for taking my scribblings and polishing them into this book!

"Note To Reader"

The story you are about to read is true. I have tried to recreate events, locales, and conversations from my memories of them. In order to maintain their anonymity, I have changed the names of individuals and places.

To enhance your reading experience I've compiled pictures, court records, and news articles onto a webpage:

https://www.40parents.com/webpage.html

TABLE OF CONTENTS

FIRST DAY IN FOSTER CARE

Age: 4
Duration: one month

On October 10, 1985, an anonymous caller phoned the police department to report about a woman with two small children. The caller said she had observed the woman slapping the oldest boy on his bare leg five times, causing redness. I was that boy.

When two child abuse specialists arrived at the lobby of Social Services they noticed my brother and I had bruises on our facial cheeks, buttocks, backs, and arms. One of them asked my mother to step outside so they could chat. My mother said she moved to town five days ago and only had $2.00. Her parents brought her to Las Vegas, but had kicked her out after the hotel management found out her kids were living there which was against motel policies. She went to the food bank earlier that day and was referred to Social Services for financial assistance.

The other specialist interviewed me. I told her my mother had hit me and that her boyfriend living in the motel with us had yelled at and bruised me. When the specialist asked about her boyfriend, my mom asked for a lawyer. My brother and I were immediately removed from our mother's care and placed in Child Protection Custody.

I don't remember anything about that day or much about the events or abuses that had occurred prior to that day. However, I do have a few memories of the facility my brother and I went to first.

We were placed in a Child Protective Services facility. Youth who lived in this facility were separated into one of six buildings called 'cottages' by their age and sex. My brother was two years younger than me, so we were placed in separate cottages and only permitted to interact with each other during group 'play times.' Once or twice a day, all the youth in the facility gathered together outside to play. I looked forward to this time of day for two reasons, first I got to spend time with my brother, and second, the large clean dumpster filled with toys for us to play with.

CHAPTER 2
LIVING WITH MY DAD

Age: 4
Duration: one month

S hortly after I was taken away from my mother, Child
Protective Services contacted my father's mother and
notified her that I was in Child Protective Custody. They
wanted to know if my father was interested in gaining
custody of me. She contacted my father who happened to
be living in Las Vegas with his new wife and informed him
of the situation.

I had very little contact with my dad since my birth
due to my mother's transient lifestyle. But my father and
his new wife were happy to have me and picked me up
from the facility. Since my brother had a different father,
he was not permitted to join me and remained at the
facility.

My dad and his wife meet with a representative from
the courts to determine what was needed to gain legal
custody of me. They were instructed to hire an attorney

and complete all the steps required by the courts. They didn't have much money and secured a $3,000 loan from a family member to hire an attorney.

At the next court hearing, the judge was concerned that my mother did not have legal representation and appointed a public attorney to assist her with the case. After the court hearing, my father's attorney told him to expect a prolonged legal battle that could cost tens of thousands of dollars. And his chances of winning were slim since fathers rarely won custody battles in Las Vegas at the time.

My father and his wife didn't have the means to fund the custody battle. So they dropped the case and I was returned to the facility. I was happy to see my brother again.

To regain custody of her children, my mother, and her boyfriend agreed to attend Parental Effectiveness Training and individual counseling to address child abuse. She also needed to prove to the courts she could maintain employment and a stable living environment for three months.

During this time she was allowed supervised visitation of her children. I have a brief memory about one of those visits. When I was alone with her, she took me to Kmart to buy me shoes. I remember being so happy to see her.

This is the only memory I have of my mother. It also may have been the last time I saw her. She never completed the requirements and the courts never heard from her again.

CHAPTER 3
FIRST EIGHT FOSTER HOMES

Ages: 4 through 6
Duration: 4 days to 14 months

After another four days at the facility, Turtle (alias chosen by my brother for this book) and I were moved to our first foster home. We lived there for about three months before we were moved to our next home. I have very few memories of that time in my life. And over the next two years, we were shuffled through a total of eight foster homes.

There is no documentation about why these placements started or ended. It was, however, the court's wishes to keep Turtle and I living together in the same places whenever possible. At times, there were no homes to take both of us. We were placed in separate homes and then moved together when a home became available to take us both.

The first memory I have of those two years was a foster mom who attempted suicide. I remember the ambulance coming to the house and my foster mom being hauled away on a stretcher.

My second memory is a teenage girl who lived in one of those homes. I remember several occasions when she rubbed candy on her private parts and then had my brother and I lick it off.

The next memory is being removed from one of those homes because the couple were having their own children and no longer wanted to care for foster children.

In the next home, I lived with a married couple who took me to their church on the weekends. I didn't like church much until that experience. I remember people singing, dancing and having food and parties after the services. I think that's where I discovered my love for soul food.

The last memory I have during that time in my life was spending a lot of time out in the desert where I built forts and caught lizards.

CHAPTER 4

THE PENCE FAMILY

Ages 6 through 9
Duration: 2 years and 10 months

Living with the Pence family was one of the few times I felt safe, stable, and loved through my entire life in Foster Care. I have many fond memories of my time with the Pence family. They lived in Henderson, Nevada in a two-story house with four bedrooms. They had a fantastic backyard. It had a hammock, fruit trees, grapevines and a small office next to the garage.

The family consisted of a middle-aged, married couple and their three daughters. Their grown daughter had a child of her own and lived nearby. Mr. Pence was a semi-truck driver who worked long days and nights. Occasionally, he was away from the family for days at a time. His wife cared for their home and two teenage daughters. The younger daughter was a bit prim and proper. The older one was a bit of a rebel.

The Big Temple

Attending church was a big part of the Pence family dynamic. We went every Sunday. We also attended the opening of a large temple that had been recently built in Las Vegas. The family was really excited to go, especially the mother and father. I was amazed by the design and structure of the building. The shape of the temple looked a bit like a castle to me. We had to wait in line for our turn to tour the temple.

When it was time to go in, my brother and I were not allowed to enter since we had not been baptized members of the church. After a bit of explaining and pleading from the parents, Turtle and I were allowed to enter the main lobby area, but not any further.

I remember feeling very confused about why my brother and I were treated differently. It felt like we weren't good enough. I couldn't understand why, especially since I went to church faithfully with the family every weekend.

The family split into two groups. The older daughter, my brother, and I walked around the lobby while the rest of the family continued to tour inside.

After the tour, we all met up again and headed on our way. There was quite a bit of discussion about the temple on the car ride home. I was also curious about what baptism was and how I could do it so I could feel whole and accepted like the rest of the family.

I was told that I wasn't allowed to be baptized since the Pence family wouldn't be my family forever and my future adoptive parents might want to baptize me into another religion.

When I heard that, I felt more unworthy. Then I thought to myself, this family would be ending, just like the rest! I was heartbroken and remember completely shutting down emotionally. The family tried to convince me that I was loved and that everything was going to be okay, but I just ignored them and stewed in my anger and confusion for a bit while accepting the fact that I was a reject!

Those feelings lasted for several days. When tensions escalated a few times, I broke things out of rage. My behavior in school was impacted as well. I wasn't nice to the teachers and my fellow students. And I got into a fistfight with one of the students.

When the father picked me up from school, he pulled me aside and said if I didn't start behaving appropriately I would be kicked out.

That confused me even more. I didn't know how to behave differently. I was scared, sad, lonely, and confused. When my brother tried to console me, I lashed out at him as well.

After a few days passed, I realized life wasn't over and gathered my senses. However, at that point, I also began masking my sadness and sorrow. When parents, teachers, and therapists asked me how I was doing, I lied and told them everything was fine. I didn't understand or know how to express my feelings at that time.

Penny The Guinea Pig

The younger daughter had a guinea pig named Penny who was reddish-brown with white splotches. Their daughter agreed to let me play with Penny in exchange for cleaning out the cage. I was full of love and excitement whenever I was with Penny, so the family let me play with her often.

On two occasions the unthinkable happened. I lost Penny. Since her favorite food was dandelions, I took her out in the backyard to feast on them. In one of the corners of the backyard, large vines grew up the fence. On occasion, that's where I took Penny to play.

One day I left Penny alone for a bit while I picked fruit from the trees. When I came back, she was gone. The family and I looked everywhere in the backyard with no luck. I was heartbroken, ashamed of myself, and feeling very guilty about my actions.

Luckily, a few days later Penny was found in the vines on the other side of the fence. Thankfully I was allowed to play with her again, but only inside the house from then on. One day, the unthinkable happened again when Penny got lost in the house. A day or so later, she was found under the couch. I was relieved.

Chex Mix For Breakfast

I did a lot of stealing while I lived in that home. The first time, I took things from the pantry full of jarred and prepackaged food. I stole the food mostly out of curiosity about how it tasted, not because I was hungry.

On one occasion, I decided to make a recipe I saw in a TV ad. I needed a box of Chex cereal and a packet of seasoning. I spotted them in the pantry, opened the box, poured the packet inside and shook it up vigorously. Then I opened the box, grabbed a handful, put it in my mouth and started to chew. It tasted terrible and I immediately spat it out.

I tried to cover my tracks by placing the box back on the shelf, hoping no one noticed. If someone did notice, I would just blame it on my brother, like I did in the past. Some time went by until it was discovered. I tried to blame it on my brother again, but this time I had left a clue. I put the box back on an upper shelf where my brother was unable to reach it. I was caught red-handed. I had to eat the creation I made for breakfast every day until it was gone.

Antique Matches

The next thing I stole was a packet of matches I found in an old chest. They were the wooden ones that strike on the side of the box. They smelled and looked old. But I was excited about having a new toy. I would sneak off to light them whenever I could. Then I started to experiment by lighting things on fire that I got from the trash.

One day, the father found the pack of matches in the garage where I hid them. He confronted me and I denied knowing anything about them. He shared that they were antiques and couldn't be replaced. And that he was upset but would get over it. I felt bad and returned other items I stole from the chest that he didn't know about.

Spray Paint Explosion

One day the father was spray painting something and I watched curiously. I was fascinated by the way the can jingled when he shook it. A few days later I wanted to see how it worked. I grabbed a can of black paint, a hammer, and a screwdriver and went to the hidden space between the back of the garage and the back wall to find out.

I placed the spray can sideways on the ground. Then I pressed the screwdriver against the side and took a swing with the hammer. After a few tries, the screwdriver pierced the can and paint forcefully spewed out in a large fountain. I was amused for a split second until I realized that it was covering the wall and me with paint. I grabbed it and turned it upside down until it stopped spewing out paint.

At that point, I realized what a terrible mistake I had made. I started to cover my tracks by grabbing the water hose and attempting to spray the paint off the wall. When that didn't work, I tried nail polish remover, paint thinner, and acetone. Eventually, I got most of it off the wall. Then I found a can of paint that matched the wall and covered whatever black was left on the wall.

But the grass and I were still covered in paint. So I used the rest of the chemical to remove as much as I could. Then I prayed no one would look at the grass until I could figure out how to fix it. I promptly hid the can in the trash and jumped in the shower where I vigorously scrubbed the paint from my body. The only paint I couldn't get off was around my knuckles and fingernails. After my shower, I secretly hid the paint and chemical-soaked clothes in the trash.

Once again, I overlooked a simple area. I didn't clean the paint off the surface of the shower. I denied that it was my fault, but my fingernails told a different story. Once I knew that I was caught I told the truth. I was put on restriction but learned an interesting lesson. Trying to hide the screw up felt like it took more work and energy than the punishment for admitting it.

The Jar Full Of Coins

Instead of giving out candy for Halloween one year, we gave out 10 pennies rolled up in aluminum foil. A few days before, the whole family gathered around the dining room table for dessert. Afterwards, a very large glass jar, full of change was dumped on the kitchen table.

We sorted through the change and made one-hundred 'penny wraps' which were actually quite fun to make. The whole family was involved and I was amazed at the mound of change on the table. It felt like we were rich!

While strapping the pennies together, I grabbed a handful and stuck them in my pocket when no one was looking. I then took a break and hid the change in a sock in my room. I repeated this two more times.

I spent the three dollars I stole on candy and popsicles the next day. After I ran out of change, I searched the parents' room while they were gone. Although one of the daughters was babysitting, she spent most of the time in her room talking on the phone. Turtle agreed to sit at the bottom of the stairs and notify me if she started heading our way.

After a bit of searching, I found the jar on the floor of a closet. I had a big smile on my face as I reached into the jar and filled my hand with coins. My mood altered quickly though when I couldn't get my hand full of coins out of the jar. Eventually, I released some of the coins from my grip and was able to get my fist out.

I filled a sock up with change until it was too heavy to carry. Then I cleaned up all the change that had spilled onto the floor. I made my way down the stairs, through the kitchen, and into my bedroom, safe and sound.

The next day I put the sock of change in my backpack and took it to school to buy popsicles and chips. I rarely had the money to buy those items, but not on that day! I bought snacks for myself and friends at every break until I ran out of change.

The Lemonade Stand

A few times a week, Turtle and I would venture to a convenience store up the street. The parents would ask us to purchase something for them. And in return, they would give us each $.25 to spend on whatever candy we desired. However, it was never enough to buy the candy bars our hearts truly desired. So I devised a plan to make some money.

I decided to sell lemonade on the corner of the street. We had everything we needed at the house except packets of powdered lemonade. So Turtle and I went to the convenience store. I asked him to get the clerks attention while I put three packets of yellow lemonade powder in my pocket and walked out the store. A few seconds later,

Turtle walked out the store and we headed home excited to make and sell lemonade.

After we mixed everything together, we carried a table, the cooler, and cups to the end of the street and set up our lemonade stand. We drew a big "25 cents" sign on a piece of paper and taped it to the table. Then waited for people to pull over. An hour later, we sold out of lemonade. I was quite surprised by how easy it was to make money.

We brought everything home and told the parents about our accomplishment. They weren't happy knowing we took their supplies without asking, but they let us keep the money which came to about five dollars.

The next day we went down to the convenience store and bought our favorite candy bars. I felt very confident about my future in that moment. If I ever need money, I could always sell lemonade again.

The Water Fountain

Most days, my brother and I walked home from school. We walked by a casino that had a water fountain on the side entrance. There was a lot of change at the bottom of the fountain. I wondered why it was in there.

To me, it was a great opportunity! I sat on the bench surrounding the fountain until I positioned myself to get the best shot at getting quarters. When the coast was clear,

I reached in and grabbed as much change as I could in one shot. Then I waited a few minutes and did it again. I stole money out of the fountain five times until I got caught.

On the last attempt, the casino security guard saw me from a distance. He yelled out something to me, I looked up, saw it was a security guard and took off running. He was quite fast but I ran across the street dodging moving cars and he stopped pursuing me. I was full of adrenaline and feeling fantastic that I escaped the guard. We continued our way home with the $2 I was able to steal that day.

Getting Home from School

Kids could take a school bus if they lived at least a mile from the school. The house I lived in was just shy of a mile away from the school.

Mrs. Pence drove all the children to school in the morning. But we were on our own for getting back home. Although some parents offered to drive us back, they weren't allowed due to state policy. Since my brother and I were wards of the state, the parents would have to undergo background checks and other inspections to drive us.

So my brother and I usually walked home from school, which I didn't mind most of the time. It was a chance for us to explore. Sometimes we went to the park and hung out there for a while before our trek home. On most days, we just walked down the main street, walked by the stores, looked at the buildings and watched people.

On hot days, we walked into the stores and asked for some water. I loved walking by the casinos. It was something about the lights, noises and the size of the buildings that continuously grabbed my attention. Although we walked in a few times, we were immediately turned away by security.

At some point, a new family moved in next door with a boy my age. We quickly became best friends. His mom gave us a ride home when she was available. She would stop at the corner so Turtle and I could get out of the car without the Pence's seeing us.

On a few occasions we stopped by a Bar on our walk home. The Bar was owned by the neighbors Grandfather. We stopped in because we were thirsty and needed water which his Grandfather gladly gave us. Then he brought us all fries and sodas. I remember feeling so excited about going there.

Then one day we got caught because we hung out a little too long. I wound up telling the truth about going to the bar and the Pence's became extremely upset. It was perhaps the most upset I ever saw them. They weren't necessarily mad at Turtle and I. They were mad at the neighbor's mom and the grandpa for allowing us into the bar in the first place. I was forbidden from playing with the neighbor boy and that made me really upset. I didn't understand why he was in trouble for the mistakes of grown-ups. So I disobeyed the order and we continued to play together in secrecy.

My First Kiss

At the far end of the street lived a girl who was one year older than me. Eventually, we became boyfriend and girlfriend. We hung out at her place on most days after school. We played and chatted about who knows what until it got dark and I headed home.

I still have a vivid memory of when I kissed her for the first time. We were on the side patio of her house and she was leaning on one of the posts. While we were talking, I leaned in quickly and kissed her. We kissed several times after that and we had sex with our clothes on while moving our hips around on top of each other. It was the best sex ever!

Her parents liked me until they found out I was a foster kid. Once they found out they forbid me from seeing her. I was heartbroken and yelled mean stuff at them when they told me to leave. She snuck out a few times to see me afterward, but eventually just ignored me when our paths crossed.

The Electric Jolt

On a warm day, the neighbor across the street set up a mini water park in his front lawn for his kids and the neighborhood children to play in.

The setup included water guns, water balloons, a kiddie pool, and a water slide. It was so much fun! I was in kiddie heaven! We played for hours on end. When it became dark, lights had been set up so the fun would continue on. I got the idea to move a light over to the water gun filling station.

As soon as I grabbed the light, I received a jolt of electricity. I wanted to let go, but I couldn't. A few seconds later, after I was able to let go, I fell to the lawn in excruciating pain. It felt like my body was on fire and a ringing noise crippled my hearing. The adults came to rescue me and gave me a lecture about not touching electric things when I have wet hands.

Chemical Plant Explosion

A small room on the side of the garage was used as an office, for storage, and my dream/play zone. I spent a lot of time in the room playing with toys and daydreaming about who knows what.

One day, I came home from school, grabbed my lunch, and headed to the playroom as usual. Then twenty minutes later, a loud explosion shattered the windows of the office. I was shocked, frightened and intrigued all at the same time. Glass was everywhere. I felt trapped and didn't know what to do.

Luckily, a few minutes later, Mrs. Pence opened the door and whisked me away to safety. First, she cleaned up my nicks and scratches. Then she investigated what had happened. There was an explosion at a nearby chemical processing plant and since we were only a few miles away, we were within its blast radius.

Chickenpox

A boy my age had red spots all over his body. Mrs. Pence insisted I play with him. He looked sick and I didn't want to.

She still insisted I play with him and made sure we touched each other and drink from the same glass. I was told she did that to make me sick, too. If I didn't do it then, I might die if I get the disease later in life. I was willing to take the risk and protested the entire time.

A few days later, I started getting red bumps all over my body. I panicked a bit until I was told I didn't have to go to school for the next few days. Then I was happy and saw it as a gift.

However, the next day the spots started itching. Mrs. Pence put a pink liquid on the red spots and it stopped the itching for a bit. Eventually, my entire body itched and she had to put socks on my hands to stop me from scratching myself. The inside of my throat itched and there was nothing I could do about it. I felt horrible!

After three days passed, the itching stopped and the spots went away. I was so happy to go back to school.

The Forbidden Boyfriend

At one point, the older daughter had a boyfriend. Since he was black, she wasn't permitted to see him. The daughter and mother fought and yelled at each other over the situation.

However, the daughter continued to date him. When her parents were gone, she would try to sneak him over to the house without Turtle and I knowing about it.

When I caught them, she made me pledge to never tell on her, and if I did, there would be a severe punishment! But that didn't work and she wound up having to bribe me.

One day, I asked her for permission to go with my friends to the fast food restaurant on the other side of the highway. I figured she wouldn't let me do that since there were no crosswalks for a few blocks and we would have to run across the freeway.

However, since I had something she wanted, I asked her anyway. When she refused as anticipated, I told her I was going to tell on her. Although she became irritated by that, she allowed me to go. However, we had to ride our bikes up to the crosswalk and cross the highway that way. The crosswalk was far beyond our two-street radius and it was quite the adventure, but we made it back home safely. I tried using that trick on her again, but It didn't work the next time.

The Birthday Tree

My best friend lived in the house to the west of us. And an old man lived in the house to the east. He didn't talk to us much and we would sneak into his yard and steal things. Eventually, we got caught by Mr. Pence and had to return everything. The old man wasn't pleased with us.

On my eighth birthday, he did something that blew my mind. He planted a large pine tree in his front yard and said it was my birthday present. I was beyond thrilled.

The family moved away from the house, but the tree still stands. Whenever I'm in that area, I like to drive by and marvel at the size of the tree and ponder about the wonderful memories created at the Pence's.

Adoptive Home

The state found a couple who were willing to adopt Turtle and I. Outings were arranged for the four of us to spend time together. After a few more meetings we went to live with them. I don't remember being very fond of the idea, but there wasn't much I could do about it.

The parents and daughter allowed me to take Penny the guinea pig with me. They said I took such could care of her that she loved me the most. That filled my heart with joy and I became excited to move to the new family.

CHAPTER 5
THE WALLEY HOME

Age: 9
Duration: 7 Months

The Walley's were a middle-aged married couple with no children of their own. They lived in a five-bedroom house with two dogs. The husband worked as an engineer in a local slot machine company. His wife was an art professor at a local college.

Turtle and I lived with them on a one-year probation period. At that time, in the state of Nevada, we were required to live with the potential adopter for one year before the state would grant legal custody.

Striking Out

The father signed me up for a season of little league and took me to all the practices and games. I remember enjoying baseball and I caught on to the game really quick.

However, I had one major flaw. I couldn't hit the ball. I was tall for my age so when it was my turn at bat, the coaches would tell the kids in the outfield to back up. I remember thinking, "Wow! They must think I'm strong."

I got up to bat and would strike out every time. I felt embarrassed and ashamed of myself.

I was fairly good at almost everything else except hitting. I worked extra hard to make up for my mistakes at-bat.

Being the catcher was my favorite position. I loved dressing up in the pads and feeling the sting of the ball hitting my hand through the padded gloves. It was far more active than standing in the outfield waiting for a ball to come. I really liked hearing the umpires yell the strikes in my ear as well.

However, there was another boy who was much better in that position then I was. He played most of the time. But if he was tired or we were playing an easy team, the coach let me play the position.

At one of the practices toward the end of the season, I finally made real contact with the ball. When I heard the crack of the bat, I looked up and could see the ball soaring. If I were in a real game, it would've been a home run. It felt so good to finally hit the ball. I ran around the bases in celebration even though it was just practice!

Big Screen TV

Living in that home was my first real introduction to sports. The father would also watch football games on the big screen TV they had in the living room. I'd only seen a big screen TV a few times so I was really happy we had one.

I remember watching the Super Bowl for the first time. It was Super Bowl XXV against the New York Giants and the Buffalo Bills. I don't remember much about the game but I do remember all the yummy food and how excited everyone was throughout the game. I believe our family was rooting for the Bills (who lost by one point.)

I also remember the Halftime Show about the Gulf War which was underway. I remember being amazed by the rockets, tanks and the stealth planes. They looked so cool. I also remember feeling a bit sad and confused about why these people were fighting in the first place.

However, I watched plenty of Gi-Joe cartoons, in which the Americans were always the Hero. So I thought they were killing bad guys and videos of the real explosions looked a lot cooler than the ones in the cartoons. I thought the fighter pilots were so cool and I wanted to be like them when I grew up.

Forts in the Desert

I continued to spend a lot of my free time outdoors. The neighborhood we lived in was still being developed. There was open desert between some of the houses. My brother and some friends from the neighborhood set up forts on the opposite sides of the lots.

We threw rocks and other items at each other. Before each battle, we spent time re-enforcing our forts with boards, logs, and anything else we could find. Then we collected a pile of rocks to throw at each other. The rocks had to be light enough to throw but heavy enough to cause damage to the fort.

Turtle was usually on my team, but he could only throw very light rocks. Although he wasn't of much assistance, when the battle began, he was great at finding rocks and keeping an eye out for incoming rocks.

Each side took turns throwing rocks at each other until one side no longer felt safe behind their structure and surrendered. Then the next day we would repeat the entire process.

The YMCA

When school was out in the summer, Turtle and I spent most of our days at the YMCA while the Walleys worked. The daily activities included sports, games, and swimming. The pool had two diving boards, a tall one and a short one. Since I couldn't swim, I wasn't allowed to go on either of them. I shared this with the Walleys one day and they signed Turtle and me up for a few swimming lessons.

It didn't take long for me to be jumping off the small diving board and having a blast. I tried the tall diving board once or twice but it was scary so I stuck with the smaller diving board. There was something about floating in the air and diving deep into the water afterward that really excited me.

Then for one week all the kids were loaded onto a bus and headed to Summer Camp. I felt scared because the last time I went on an adventure like that, I got lost at Disneyland. Although I didn't want to go, early next morning we showed up at the YMCA. The parents put my sleeping bag and suitcase in a compartment under the bus and basically forced me to get on the bus.

Once we got to our camping site, I was pretty happy to be there. There was a lake you could go fishing in. I was super excited to go out on one of the canoes and go fishing. But I would have to rent the fishing gear which would have taken all of the ten dollars the parents gave me for the trip. So I passed on that activity and saved my money for candy and other treats.

All the kids took turns participating in different activities including horseback riding, archery, and arts and crafts to name a few.

I really hit it off with one of the girl campers and we decided to be boyfriend and girlfriend. We hung out at breaks and even made each other arts and crafts.

Selling Sports Trading Cards

Among a few other things, the Walley's gave me a box of sports cards for Christmas. The box contained 25 individually wrapped packets of 10 cards. I brought the cards to the YMCA to show them off and to trade them.

One of the boys took advantage of me. He took all my good cards and gave me ones that were worthless. Eventually one of the other kids told me what he was up to. I confronted him and he told me it was my fault because I made the trades.

I also told one of the staff members, and they told his parents. They were willing to give the cards back to me. The next day, they brought all of his cards and asked me to tell them which ones were mine.

I didn't know exactly what cards I had traded him. He took advantage of this, I found one that I thought we traded, he claimed he got it from someone or someplace else. In the end, I did get a few cards back. And I learned from the experience that certain cards have value, and certain people will take advantage of the unsuspecting.

One weekend I decided to sell my cards to the other kids to make some money. I carried a table and chair to the corner of the street. Then I wrote, "Football Cards for Sale" on a few pieces of paper and taped them to light poles around the block.

Business was slow at first, so I put up some more signs. This time I also taped a real card to the pole as well. When some kids came by, I let them name their own price and I sold a few dollars' worth of cards.

Then a boy came up to me holding one of the cards I had taped against the light pole. At first, I was a bit angry because he took it down. Then he explained that the card was rare and he would have given me $10 to $20 dollars for it. Excitedly, I asked him why he didn't give me the money now.

He said I ruined the card by taping it and that it was now worthless. He also looked through the rest of my cards and said they weren't worth anything. Out of frustration, I sold him the rest of the cards for $5.

Stealing from Church

We went to Church most Sundays. The parents gave Turtle and I a few dollars to put in the collection bowl that was passed around each week. I did as I was asked the first few times. Then one week, I decided to pretend like I was putting the money in the bowl, but I put it back in my pocket instead.

Since it worked, I continued until I got caught. The parents bought piggy banks as gifts for my brother and me. After church, I would sneak back to my room and add the money to whatever was already in my piggy bank.

Then one day, I wanted to buy a new toy. When the parents told me I couldn't do that, I jokingly said I could use my own money. Then brought my piggy bank to them with $10 to $20 in it and asked if I had enough. They were quite shocked and asked how I got the money.

I couldn't tell them that I was stealing it from church, so I told them I was saving it from the time I sold my sports cards. They were quite impressed and took me to the store to buy the toy.

Eventually, they dropped the amount they gave us to give to the church to $1. That's when I tried a different approach. I put my $1 in the bowl, but I took out $2 to $5 back out. I got away with it a few times and then I got caught by one of the people sitting next to me.

The Walleys were pretty upset and were convinced that this was how I was getting my money, which was correct. They took my piggy bank away with all the money in it. They also took the toy I bought away. I became quite upset and started slamming doors. I even knocked one of the mother's cherished paintings off the wall and caused damage.

10th Birthday

Every day I rode my bike to and from school. One day, it was special. It was my birthday. I rode my bike home with excitement. I was ready to eat cake and open new presents.

However, when I arrived, a strange car from the state was in the driveway. I could tell it was from the state because all the cars looked the same. They also had the state's logo painted on the door. Every time I was in one of those cars, it meant I was going to go to a new home.

When I walked into the house, the parents and a person from the state were standing by the door. All of my belongings were being packed into large white trash bags.

At that point, I got pretty angry and violent. My brother started to cry and asked me to stop, so I did.

Then I was in the backseat of the car, crying and traveling to a new home. My brother stayed with the Walleys who eventually adopted him.

CHAPTER 6

THE CHILDREN'S HOME

Age: 10 through 11
Duration: 13 months

In a small city outside of Las Vegas was a youth facility run by the State of Nevada. This facility housed approximately 40 foster youth, ages 5-17. The facility consisted of seven homes in a semi-secluded area. Four homes were for boys and three were for girls.

The facility also contained a basketball court, football field, handball court, and a few other buildings.

When I arrived at my new home, the family was seated around a large table eating dinner. They offered me a plate but I wasn't very hungry. After dinner, they tried to cheer me up with a birthday cake and a few presents. But I was still quite sad, angry, confused, and scared.

The "House Parents" tried their best to welcome me, but all I wanted to do was be myself. The parents needed

35

to go over the rules and regulations of living there. But I could care less. I just wanted to go to my room.

They informed me that it wasn't permitted until they went over everything. That included having my belongings searched.

One of the parents went through my belongings and wrote down everything I owned on a piece of paper. Although I wasn't allowed to have some of my things anymore (slingshot, money, etc.), I was told that the staff would hold onto those belongings until I moved from the facility, or until I turned 18.

A few months later, two of the kids in the home broke into the closet where the confiscated belongings were stored. I was pretty upset, especially when the staff told me they wouldn't replace any of the stolen items.

However, if I wanted to get my stuff back, I would have to tell them who took it. I already knew that two of the older boys in the home did it. The boys said that if I told anyone, they would beat me up. That would have been worse than losing a slingshot and any other possession.

A few weeks later, one of the other older boys who lived in the complex was playing with a slingshot which looked just like mine. When I asked him where he got it, he said, "The store."

I knew it was mine. But there was nothing I could really do about it, and he could have easily beaten me up if I tried to take it away from him.

Besides that, if I had told on him, the consequences would have been even worse, both physically and socially.

The Nickel Arcade

Once a month the parents took us on a family outing. We would load up in one of the vans and drive for about 45 minutes to our first stop, a fast food restaurant. The house parents ordered a meal for themselves and bought us all a cup for soda. After we got the cup, we were allowed to have all the soda we could drink for about an hour.

Anyone who had their own money could buy food as well. One time, when I bought some fries, the other kids asked me for some. Since I wasn't comfortable turning them down at that point, only a few of the fries wound up in my belly.

The next part of the trip was my favorite. We drove another 45 minutes to a Casino in Jean, NV. The vans were pretty large, with four rows of seats, not including the driver and front passenger seats. I got picked on if I sat in any other row except the first row. The kids behind me plucked my ears, pulled my hair, and stuck their wet fingers in my ear. When I turned around to see who was doing that, they all acted like nothing happened.

Eventually, I just sat in the front row. Their behavior didn't stop completely but it was much better than being in the back. It was a small price to pay for the fun I was about to have.

When we arrived at the casino, the house parent escorted us to the arcade area. Every game cost a nickel each.

The parents gave each of us a $2 roll of nickels to play while they gambled in the casino. An hour later, one of the house parents gave us each another half roll of nickels to continue playing. I was pretty good at managing my nickels. I only played a few games that I played well and lasted the longest.

By the end of the night, I usually had a few nickels to spare. I gave some to the other kids who ran out of them. They promised to pay me back the next time. Some did, and some didn't. However, I wouldn't give them any more nickels if they didn't pay me back. I stuck to my word on that one.

Eventually, the house parents got fired for some reason, and our trips to the unlimited soda fountain and arcade ended.

Free Tapes

The home had many magazines for us to read. One day, I saw an advertisement in a magazine offering seven new cassette tapes for only one dollar. I remember feeling like that was incredible offer. So I read the directions and did what it said.

I tore out the page, filled in my name and address with a pen, and then selected seven of the bands that were listed. I asked the house parents for an envelope, a stamp, and one dollar of my money they were saving for me.

They asked me what I needed it for. I told them I was going to send a letter and the dollar as a present to my brother. When they agreed, I put my selections and the dollar in the envelope and mailed it off. A few weeks later a package showed up. I had never received a package before. I was super excited to see what was inside.

When I opened it up, I found three of the cassettes that I had listed along with a letter that said in order to get the other four tapes, first I had to buy four more tapes at the price of $12 each. I felt a bit tricked. I had either ignored or didn't actually read that part of the advertisement.

Later that day, one of the house parents asked me what I received. I showed them the three tapes. Since one of the tapes had curse words on it, they took it away from me.

After that, once a month for the next few months, I received a letter from the same company reminding me that I had free tapes waiting for me after I purchased the other four.

My Best Friend

When I was in the fifth grade, I became friends with Jared, a boy my age. I'm not sure how we became friends, but I was lucky we did. Jared lived with his mother and grandparents in an RV which was in an RV Park a few miles from the school.

After school, we went on adventures around the RV Park, hunting lizards and exploring the desert. The park was right next to railroad tracks. There were a few antique train cars on the track which stayed in the same spot. For some reason, I was always intrigued by the train tracks and cars.

Jared's aunt managed a local dry cleaning store which was on the other side of the tracks. So we would often stop and say hello to her, usually because she gave us a few dollars to help her sort and iron clothes. Then we spent the money on root beer floats.

Jared and his family accepted me as one of their own. They always invited me over to play whenever I was allowed to.

One day, Jared and I got into a fight at school. I'm not sure why I punched him in the face during recess one day, but when he wouldn't punch me back, I got really sad and started to cry. I believe I was starting to get close to Jared and his family and I tried to push them away out of Survival. I didn't want to get hurt again. When the grandfather pulled us together to have chat, thankfully we were able to let bygones be bygones.

After Jared forgave me, I promised not to do it again and our friendship continued. Until one day when it was time for him to go back to Montana with his mom. That devastated me. I cried for two days after he left town. Although his grandparents stayed in town and invited me over, it just wasn't the same without Jared.

His aunt and uncle were interested in adopting me. I visited their home on the weekends. They were pretty cool and I was happy about potentially living with them. Then I got into some legal trouble and they no longer wanted to adopt me. It upset me and broke my heart.

Lizard Hunting

I spent most of my free time wandering the desert which surrounded the Children's Home. I didn't feel loved or accepted by the parents or the kids living in the home, so the desert was my escape mechanism. I would hunt for lizards and just explore. I had no clue about what I was exploring, but I would do it day after day until it got dark.

The Three Brothers

When the house parents in the first home were fired, the boys who were living in the home were divided up and placed in the remaining cottages.

The entire time I lived at this facility there were three brothers who had it out for me. Two of the brothers were a few years younger than me. I was moved into the home where the older brother and the youngest brother were living.

Things were fine until the day I told on the older brother for stealing something of mine. From that point on, the brothers went out of their way to make my life miserable and my life became a nightmare.

After the older brother beat me up for telling on him, I was in constant fear. They also told other kids in the facility not to be my friend. I was an outcast and there was nothing I could do about it.

Anytime I told the staff, the three brothers would tell a different story. At that point, I just went along with whatever they said or did. I felt trapped and just wanted to be accepted by them and the other kids in the facility.

During the summer, we were required to spend our days at the local recreation center. There was very little supervision in the pool and a park. One day, the older brother convinced me to smoke a cigarette. I told him and the other kids that I wasn't interested. But he kept calling me names and told me he would beat me up if I didn't smoke. When I took a puff, I started to cough.

Fortunately, he and the other kids were nice to me after that. So I was glad I smoked the cigarette. Then they invited me to partake in other activities.

One day, on our way home from the recreation center, the older brother and a few of the other older kids decided to break into a house.

Although I didn't want to be involved, they told me that if I left, they would beat me up. So I stayed on the lookout. My job was to tell them if anyone was coming up the alley so they could get out safely.

Since no one came, after a few minutes, they returned from the house and we all went on our merry way. Although I don't recall what they stole, I do recall them telling me that I would be beaten up if I told on them.

A few days later, a policeman came to the house and interviewed us about the break-in. I don't recall what I told the police officer, but he handcuffed me and the older brother. Then he placed us into his police car. A few minutes later, we were released with a warning. Since the brothers were being nice to me, I kept going along with them.

Another day the older brother convinced me to skip the first period of class with him. I had never skipped class before. However many of the other kids at school would talk about their adventures skipping class. I was intrigued to find out what it was like.

Our destination was a water tower on top of a hill near the school. Other kids in school would talk about their adventures at the water tower so I was very curious. It probably took us an hour or so to walk up to the tower.

When we got up on the top of the tower I was thrilled. The view was fantastic. One side overlooked the city and the other side overlooked Lake Mead. We decided to skip the rest of school that day and walk down to the Lake Marina.

It took us a few more hours to walk down to the marina through the desert. But when we got there I was thrilled. Large schools of carp came up to the dock when popcorn or bread had been thrown into the water. Hundreds of fish gathered tightly, hoping to get a bite. There were so many fish that some would end up out of water on top of the other fish. That amazed me.

We watched it happen for an hour or so until someone gave us a bag of popcorn to feed the fish. I tried to spread the popcorn out so that all the fish could eat. Then the older brother threw some popcorn in one area, and when the fish came up to eat, he punched the fish. I gave it a shot but it hurt my heart. So, I stuck with my method of fish feeding, while he continued his.

Although we planned to return to school before the end of our classes, we continued to hang out at the marina until the sun started to set. At that point, we decided to walk back. We made it about halfway when we came across a ranger station.

At that point, it was pitch black and we were hungry, thirsty, and exhausted. So I picked up the phone and told the ranger who answered, that we had skipped school and couldn't find our way home. An hour later, one of the staff at the facility picked us up in one of the facility vans.

Since we were expecting a park ranger, we were a bit shocked and nervous when the white van pulled up. The staff member made sure we knew how much trouble we were in and notified us that we would be grounded. Over the next few weeks, we did extra chores and wrote essays about why what we did was wrong.

Breaking My Arm

At lunchtime, a friend and I would play after we finished eating our meals. One day we decided to play tug of war with my arm. As my friend pulled from one end, I pulled with my body. We were playing on the stage in the lunch area. He was positioned on the stage while I was positioned on one of the steps leading up to the stage.

After the battle started, within a few minutes, he released his grip and I fell to the floor using my hand to break the fall. Many people who were eating lunch rushed over to see if I was okay. Although I told them I was fine, they could see a bone in my arm protruding from under my skin. When I looked down, I saw what they could see.

It didn't hurt until I looked down and saw that my bone was broken and then the pain rushed in. I was taken to the nurse's office and waited for one of the staff members to take me to the hospital.

When I arrived at the hospital, x-rays were taken which verified the broken bone in my forearm. The doctor snapped my bone back into place and wrapped a cast around it. Then I got to choose the color of my cast which I thought was pretty cool. After it dried 30 minutes later, I was told that I needed to do things differently over the next few months.

I had to keep the cast and skin around it as clean as possible. I was supposed to wrap the cast in plastic anytime I took a shower or was near water. If it itched, I was not supposed to stick anything down my cast. I failed at all three.

I continued to play in the dirt. A few times, water got into the bags which I fitted around the cast in the shower. I continuously inserted long branches and coat hangers in the cast to stop the itching on my arm.

On one occasion, a pencil got stuck inside the cast. When the cast was finally removed, my arm was pale, skinny, and smelled bad. The pencil left a small indention on my arm for a few weeks.

Then it was time for physical therapy. I needed to relearn how to use my wrist. Although it was very painful, after a few weeks of physical therapy I was just like new!

Free Lunch

As a foster youth, I received free lunches at school. I was restricted to eating certain items or meals. I usually had to tell the person collecting the money for lunches that I was in that special program. Then they had to find my name on a list while the other children waited behind me. The process was a reminder every day that I was not like the other kids. I was a bit ashamed and embarrassed to go through that process every day, especially when other kids would ask me if I was poor.

Sometimes I preferred telling them I was poor rather than tell them I was an unwanted and rejected kid with no parents who loved me. I didn't quite understand what I was going through myself, let alone how to share that news with others.

I also remember acting out a bit at lunchtime to compensate for the sense of loss I felt inside. Sometimes, if I were eating with a new friend or group of friends, I skipped lunch altogether to save myself the embarrassment of telling my new friends that I lived in Foster Care.

Girlfriends

I had three girlfriends while I lived there. One lived at the facility and two others lived with their parents. Sonya was my age and the youngest of three sisters who lived at the facility as well. I enjoyed her company and felt the love in her heart.

We were good friends. One day, we decided to be boyfriend and girlfriend. We kissed a couple of times and held hands as we played after school. When some of the other kids in the facility start teasing her about being my girlfriend, she broke up with me. I was a bit heartbroken, especially because she wouldn't be my friend anymore.

The next girl had a horse at a horse boarding facility. I joined her after class so I could care for and ride the horse. I wasn't allowed to ride the horse according to the state's rules, but she broke the rules and allowed me to ride a few times.

I loved being around her and her horse. I'm not sure why we stopped hanging out, but we did. I probably felt myself getting close to her, so out of survival, pushed her away.

My third girlfriend, Amy, was a bit of a rebel, which I liked. We hung out after school. Although I don't remember all the things we did, I do remember that I received a Miami Dolphins jacket from her for Christmas.

One of the older boys who lived in the same home also liked the Dolphins, so I adopted them as my team as well. One day after school, it was cold, so I gave Amy my jacket to wear. Although I didn't mind, some of the older boys started making fun of me for giving her my jacket. They called her a slut and said she was using me. Following their advice, I broke up with Amy and took my jacket back.

Afterwards, I felt horrible about doing that. Although I really liked Amy, I liked not being picked on even more.

Talking To Turtle

I was allowed to continue interacting with my brother while I was living there. We talked on the phone about once a month and I wrote letters to him. His parents brought him out to see me a few times. I was still pretty mad at them for kicking me out, so I'm sure the interactions weren't the best for them.

Summertime

When school was out for the summer, all the kids were required to spend the day at the recreation center in town. The staff packed us a lunch and told us not to come home until the center closed.

The recreation center had a pool and a park. I loved playing in the pool. When I wasn't playing in the pool, I stayed in the park by myself. I was happy to be away from the other kids observing the interactions from a safe distance.

The Facility Shutting Down

The State of Nevada provided the financial resources to cover the operation of the facility. One of the years when the state had financial issues, they were seriously contemplating shutting down the facility as well as a similar one in Northern Nevada.

We kids learned about it on the nightly news. Most of us cheered this on. We were thrilled at the possibility that we would no longer have to live in that hell hole.

We had no idea where we would go, but we figured it couldn't be much worse than that place. Boulder City was a small town with less than 15,000 people. The kids who lived at that facility were viewed as misfits and troublemakers by the residents of the town. At least that's how I felt. We most likely earned some of that reputation given the break-ins, fights, and other trouble we had caused in the town.

Whenever I told town residents (such as parents, teachers, etc.) that I lived in the facility, many of them instantly changed their attitude and demeanor towards me. Some took pity, while others judged and distanced themselves from me. If the facility shut down, I would be happy no longer being among the black sheep.

Charity Events

Several groups of adults coordinated events specifically for youth in the facility. In the summertime, a group had a picnic for us. During the winter, a group took us Christmas caroling and another group brought us presents.

I really enjoyed Christmas caroling. We went to the hospital, retirement homes and other places just to sing for the residents. I also enjoyed providing joy to the people we sang for. Their camaraderie and energy were great.

Although I enjoyed getting presents at some of the events, we had to interact with the people who gave us the presents. I hated having to be all prim and proper. I assume the purpose of the events was to provide us with joy. However, since we weren't allowed to act like kids, it seemed like it was more for the people who were putting on the events than for us. I really hated all the questions people asked. They wanted to know why I was in the facility in the first place, and then came the pity along with it.

Eventually, I learned to use that pity to manipulate adults and kids. Essentially I learned that if I laid out a sad enough story or played the victim, people gave things or felt really sorry for me, which felt pretty good.

One year, for Christmas, all the youth boarded buses and headed to Las Vegas. A large clothing store gave each of us a $100 shopping spree. They closed the store for two hours and we had it all to ourselves. The other youth and I were thrilled as we walked around and picked out clothes to purchase with the $100 gift card.

We chatted and conferred with each other about our clothing choices. At the end of the shopping spree, I went home with a couple of pairs of pants, some t-shirts, and a sweater.

The Baritone Horn

In my first year of Junior High, I was put into band class. I had issues with some of the other students in one of the classes, so they put me into the band class. Since most of the instruments were already taken, I was stuck with the Baritone Horn.

That large instrument weighed about twenty-five pounds with the case. I had to carry it about a half a mile to and from school every day. Since the facility was perched on a steep hill, it was quite a trek, especially during the hotter months. I had to leave early so I could get to school on time.

Although the school had an extra Baritone Horn, which I could have left at home, the facility wasn't willing to pay the deposit required by the school. A few months into the class, I got fed up lugging that big ol' thing around. After I said I was going to quit, the teacher talked to the school administrators who waived the deposit requirement. I was finally allowed to bring the extra instrument home. Boy, was I relieved!

Twirler Team

One day the entire school was called into the gymnasium for a show which was put on by a group of traveling teenage students. The show was an acrobatic presentation which was incorporated with lights and music. My favorite part was when the students did somersaults and flips while a strobe light went off in the background. When it looked like they were moving in slow motion, I was mesmerized.

After the show was over, the person who managed the show told us what the youth had to do to be in the show. They had to practice many hours a day while maintaining their grades. He shared some contact information if any of the youth in the audience were interested in joining the team.

That was the first time I knew what I wanted to do with my life. I wanted to learn how to be a twirler like those youth and go around the country performing for others. A day or so later, I called the number. It was a recorded message informing me about the program and the requirements for joining the team.

One of them was that you had to be an experienced twirler. I asked my house parents how to do this and they said I would need to join a gymnastics team. There was one in town and I visited them once to check it out. It looked like a lot of work but I was up to it. There was also a fee to join and continue participating in the gymnastics training. Since the fee was more than the facility or state was willing to pay, I had to put that dream on hold.

CHAPTER 7
CHILDREN'S BEHAVIORAL SERVICES

Age: 11
Duration: 3 months

After spending thirteen months at the Children's Home, I became very depressed, withdrawn, and started to disobey the staff. They placed me in a behavioral facility two days before Thanksgiving.

That place was truly a nightmare. They required me to take drugs. When I refused, the staff tackled me to the ground, put me in a straightjacket, injected something into me and locked me in a padded room until I was ready to cooperate.

That happened on multiple occasions. I was in that facility for three months until I finally caved in, obeyed the staff and was allowed to move back to the Children's home.

CHAPTER 8
THE CHILDREN'S HOME *(PART 2)*

Age: 11 through 12
Length: 10 Months

Digging Trenches

One day, the director of the Children's Home called me into his office to offer me a job. The work involved building a ditch to water the large trees in the desert surrounding the property. He offered to pay me $2.50 an hour for my work and I gladly accepted.

For the next month, I spent my free time digging a ditch, twelve inches wide by twelve inches deep in between twenty trees. Then I dug a trench around each tree with a standard shovel. I documented my hours on a piece of paper and turned it in at the end of each week. Although the dirt was very hard and full of rocks, it gave me something to do. I also liked knowing I was able to help the trees get water. After I finished digging all the ditches, I turned on the water and watched the water flow to each tree in amazement. I continued to water the trees every week from that point on.

The Landscaping Job

I got a job doing landscaping at mobile home park. I was at some event, talking to the manager of the park. I shared that I recently dug a bunch of trenches and she offered me a job on the weekends pulling weeds, planting flowers and other tasks for a few hours a day. I was filled with joy and excitement on my first day of work. It was hard work, but at the end of the weekend she made me lunch and gave me $40. I was beyond thrilled and excited for the next weekend. I continued the job for a few weeks until all the tasks were done.

On my last day, I walked around the park and admired the work I'd done. The park was clean and well-landscaped. The manager was very happy about my work and said she would let me know if she had more work for me in the future. When she called me a few months later to help out, I had a football game that day, so I had to pass.

Flag Football

One of my favorite after-school activities was playing flag football. There was a league in the city and I was allowed to join it. I was really good, too. I was tall for my age, had great reflexes and was very competitive. I could play every position and usually played quarterback. I looked forward to practices and attended every game. It was fun even when my team lost.

Getting Arrested

One day, the older brother asked me if I wanted to "get my dick sucked with him." He led me into a bedroom where one of the younger kids who lived in the cottage was sitting on the bed. He closed the door, dropped his pants and the boy put his mouth on the older brother's private parts. Then he said it was my turn. I told him, no, but he said If I didn't do it he would beat me up. So I agreed, dropped my pants, and the kid put his mouth on my penis.

A few minutes later we pulled our pants up and we left the room. But before we did, the older brother told me and the kid that if we told anyone he would beat us up. Then he gave the kid a toy that he promised him. After that, the older brother was nice to me. He even told the younger brothers to stop picking on me. I finally felt accepted.

A few days later, he invited me to do it again. This time I was more open to it and enjoyed the intimacy and secrecy. Then one day I decided to do it on my own without the older brother and one of the staff walked in.

The next day, while at school, I was called into the principal's office. A police officer was there and wanted to interview me. She asked me questions and I denied everything like the older brother had instructed me to do.

Later that night, the older brother and I were arrested at the home. We were placed in the back of a police car and taken to juvenile detention.

Although we were told not to talk to each other, the older brother kept asking me what I told the police officer. I told him that I denied it like he instructed me to do. The police officer told us to be quiet again or there would be consequences. So I just ignored him after that.

Chapter 9
Juvenile Detention

Age: 12
Length: 1 Month

The older brother and I rode handcuffed in the back of police car for about 45 minutes to the Juvenile Detention Center. My wrists, arms, and shoulders were in incredible pain. I told the officer about the pain during the trip, but he said it was too bad and that I shouldn't have done those horrible things I did to get arrested. Eventually, my hands and arms went numb for the rest of the trip.

When we arrived to the facility, he unlocked one of my handcuffs and locked it to the chair where I sat for the next thirty minutes while he filled out the paperwork. Feelings started to come back to my hands and arms. The wrist that was free had a deep red gouge from the pressure of the handcuffs.

Other youth who were already in the cells were banging on the doors, and yelling obscene language. The guards yelled at them to "Shut the fuck up!" Eventually, they went into one of the rooms and restrained one of the youth. I could hear the youth screaming from where I was sitting.

The older brother sat there like it wasn't a big deal. I sat there and cried my eyes out. I was so afraid, confused and felt completely helpless. What was I going to tell my new potential adoptive parents? Would they still love me, or was I going to be locked in this scary place forever?

Twenty minutes later, it was my turn to be processed. I was taken into a bathroom with one of the guards and told to take off all my clothes. After he searched through my clothing while I stood there naked, he told me to turn my back to him, bend over, touch my toes, and cough three times. I was crying so bad that I could barely catch my breath to cough. He was checking to see if I had anything in my butt. I felt so vulnerable and humiliated.

After I put out my clothes back on I was given two thin blankets and placed in one of the ten locked rooms within that part of the facility. I was told that I would remain there until the morning and the door was locked shut.

Luckily I was placed in the cell by myself due to being twelve years old and my crimes. The room was approximately 6'x10' and contained a single metal bench along the wall with a metal toilet and sink in the corner.

The room was sealed by a large metal door with a long, bulletproof window about 6"x 2 feet in length.

When I first arrived in the room, I felt a bit relieved for some reason. I placed my two blankets on the bench and just sat there for about twenty minutes. I was happy about not being in the same room with any of the other youth and felt relatively safe.

After I gathered my senses and stopped crying, I used the bathroom and drank some water out of the sink. Graffiti was etched into almost all the metal in the room. I spent the next thirty minutes scanning all the graffiti. It was mainly the names of gangs, gang members, and messages of hate.

Then I stood at the door and looked out the window at the other youth as they came in and out of the facility. At some point, I decided to lie on the bench. The bench and the room were really cold. Eventually, I dozed off.

Next thing I knew, the door was unlocking and then opened. An older youth wearing an orange jumpsuit walked in and placed a tray of food on the floor. Then the door was locked again. The meal consisted of eggs, grits, toast, and a small carton of milk. It also came with a package of butter, sugar and a plastic fork. I ate the food quickly and went back to sleep. I could escape the situation momentarily if I just went back to sleep.

Then twenty minutes later, I heard the door unlock and another older youth in an orange jumpsuit walked in and picked the tray up off the ground. I tried to go back to sleep with no luck.

I re-read the graffiti and looked out the window again. Then a few hours later, the door unlocked again and I was told to come out of the room.

There was a new guard who escorted me back to the main part of the facility.

The walk took about ten minutes. As we walked, he asked me what I was in for. I said, "sexual assault." When he asked me what I did, I told him. He told me to not tell that story to any of the other youth or they would beat me up. All of a sudden, all my fears returned.

He suggested that I make up another story. I told him that I was once arrested for accessory to burglary. He said I should tell other kids that I was there for that reason, to just stay to myself and not talk to any of the other kids in the detention center.

When I arrived in the main facility, there were twenty to thirty kids and they were all dressed the same.

They were watching TV, doing chores and playing games like cards, dominoes, etc. I was given new clothes and escorted to the bathroom to take a shower. The guard told me to take off all my clothes in front of him and wash with a special soap. I think it was lice soap.

Then he handed me my new clothes which matched everyone else. After getting dressed, I sat at a table and was told to stay there since I would be going to court soon. Most of the youth were much older and physically bigger than me. Many had tattoos. I was pretty scared. When the youth next to me asked why I was there, I told him my fake story. However, the paper I was given listed my real charges. So I curled the paper up and stuck it under my leg so no one else could see it.

Thirty minutes later, three more guards walked up to the table with chains and handcuffs. One by one, we were placed in the restraints consisting of a chain wrapped around our waists and padlocked. Handcuffs were placed around our wrists. There was also a longer chain which went down to our feet with additional handcuffs which then wrapped around our ankles.

After everything was connected, I could only lift my arms a few inches from my side. And the ankle cuff only allowed me to take one small step at a time. It took a bit of time to get used to walking like that. If my nose itched, I had to bend my head down to my hands to itch it.

Five youth from our building were escorted to join the youth from the other buildings. There were about twenty altogether. We walked in a single file line through a set of underground hallways which were made of concrete and smelled like mildew. I can still remember the loud sound of the doors closing that echoed and shook the hallways as we went from one to another.

After we arrived in the court area, we were placed in a room with seats along the walls and a TV playing. There was enough seating that many of us had empty seats between us.

I used that time to look at the paper given to me earlier. I read it with a conscious effort to make sure no one else could read it. I didn't understand most of it, so I read it a few times and then put it away.

Twenty minutes later, a guard entered the room and said my name. When I raised my hand (as far as I could), he told me to come with him. I was escorted to another room where a man in a suit sat at a table, with a stack of folders in front of him. He asked me to have a seat, introduced himself and said he was my public defender.

When he asked me if I understood what was going on, I said that I didn't. He explained my charges and that I would enter a plea of guilty or not guilty that day. I told him I wasn't guilty. I continued to deny everything and blamed it all on the older brother while I cried the entire time.

I was escorted back to the waiting room by one of the guards. Twenty minutes later, a guard came back in and called my name again. This time I was escorted into the courtroom. It looked familiar because I had been there a few times before when I was dealing with my family stuff.

However, this was the first time I was there in handcuffs. As soon as I entered the room, I started crying again. A few minutes later, the judge asked me how I plead and I said, "Not guilty." Then he had a conversation with other people in the room. An additional court date was set and they talked about where I would stay until then.

One of the adults said I could not go back to the Children's Home because the two youth I assaulted still lived there and would have to find other arrangements. Three weeks later, I was released from juvenile detention. I was relieved to be free again, but scared about what home I was headed to next.

CHAPTER 10
EMERGENCY YOUTH CARE CENTER

Age: 12
Duration: 2 months

The next facility served multiple purposes. It housed runaway youth, youth receiving drug and alcohol treatment, and an emergency shelter for youth who were wards of the state, on probation, or on parole.

The youths were separated into different sections of the facility depending on the reason they were there. Youth commingled during the day in the common areas and were only separated at bedtime. However, with little supervision, the youth were able to sneak in and out of their rooms throughout the night. They were also able to sneak away during the day to have sex, smoke cigarettes, and use drugs.

The facility was in one of the worst parts of the city. Drug dealers, pimps, and gang members were a regular sight on the street outside of the facility which wasn't locked. The windows and doors were fitted with sensors to notify staff if they were open. It was pretty easy to disconnect or rig the sensors, so youth came in and out as they pleased.

During the day, I attended the local middle school in the area. It was predominantly a black neighborhood, so I stood out as a white child when I walked to and from school.

The facility also housed young girls who were arrested for prostitution. The pimps waited outside for the girls to sneak out to them. As I left the facility for school, the pimps walked next to me and asked questions about who was in the facility. The drug dealers asked me if I wanted drugs while others stared at me with unkindness in their eyes. I always felt scared going to and from school. I found a pointed weapon on the street and carried it in my pocket in case I had to defend myself.

I felt like an outcast at the school. I was one of just a few white kids. The other students called me a cracker and other mean names. Fortunately, a black girl became my friend. We sat together during lunchtime and played during the breaks. I was so grateful for her.

The other youth in the facility found out what I was arrested for from the staff. They picked on me continuously. They said, "Hey, Fagot," or "Child

Molester," when they wanted to get my attention. I usually ignored them and stuck to myself. That really hurt my feelings. I felt so lonely, scared, hopeless and lost.

My brother's parents also told me that I couldn't talk to him anymore. When they found out I had been arrested, they told me he was no longer my brother and to stop calling him. I didn't listen though and continued to call. When I did, they just ignored my calls.

At that point in life, I felt so defeated, lonely and scared. I was tired of being hurt. I felt like there was no one I could trust or connect with. I felt so weak. I just shut down emotionally out of a sense of survival. I had been abandoned by everyone I loved. I just accepted that no one loved me. I stopped loving myself and started building a wall around my heart to protect myself from the world.

CHAPTER 11
JUVENILE DETENTION *(PART 2)*

Age: 12
Duration: 4 months

Prior to my trial, the older brother admitted to committing the crimes while I pleaded my innocence. Then the two youth took the witness stand and explained what occurred while I sat there and cried.

After a few days of overwhelming evidence, the judge found me guilty of two felony counts of sexual assault. Then the judge ordered the bailiff to handcuff me so I could be held in juvenile detention until sentencing.

A week later, I went before the judge for my sentencing. At that point, I could care less about what happened to me. I had no hope for the future and everyday was a fight for survival mentally and emotionally

The prosecutor made his case: I was a menace to society and deserved the maximum punishment available. I lied to the the courts, showed no remorse, and was resistant to authority. The judge sentenced me to six months in a juvenile correctional facility and three years of Parole.

At that moment, I wholeheartedly accepted that I was an unlovable menace to society and that I was doomed to a life of pain and misery.

There was a three-month waiting list to get into the specific detention center I was sentenced to. And it was where the worst kids went. So if I were going to survive, I needed to learn how to be mean, manipulative, and aggressive quickly.

I listened to other kids share their stories about being mean, manipulative and aggressive. Then I internalized those lessons and stories for use later.

I no longer allowed others to pick on me. When they did, I unleashed the rage building up inside me. However, since I started crying instantly, I became known as the kid who cried when he got into an argument or fight.

I was still a scrawny, twelve-year-old in a facility full of hardened teenagers, so most of the time I avoided physical altercations.

However, I learned how to take verbal abuse without it hurting me. I also learned how to manipulate the guards and other youth to get what I wanted.

It was still essential that I didn't let anyone know what I was arrested for. So I continued to hone my story and re-built my image so I could bond with the other youth in detention.

I told lies of being in gangs, committing crimes and not getting caught, using drugs and mistreating women. Whenever other youth didn't believe me or found discrepancies in my stories, I changed my stories so they were more interesting and believable.

I still had a cell to myself while the other youth were two or more to a cell. Whenever I felt threatened or like I was in over my head, I just acted up so I would be locked in my cell and away from the others.

There were a few saving graces for me. The first was we were allowed to have books in our cells. I read the bible completely through twice. I didn't understand it much, but I lost myself in the stories, trying to figure out what they meant. I also read fiction books. They allowed me to escape my pains and sorrows, briefly.

The second respite was my art teacher. On Tuesdays and Thursdays, we went to art class for an hour. The teacher taught us how to draw and paint.

She was such a sweet, loving person who melted me and the other youths hardened exteriors. She didn't see us as criminals. She just saw us as kids. I was so grateful for her. Twice a week she reminded me of love, kindness, compassion, and acceptance.

Fear of Showers

Quite a bit of bullying and fighting occurred during shower time. It was one of the rare occurrences that the youth could interact with each other without the supervision of the guards. So if bullying or threatening needed to be done, that was the time to do it. Some of the youth brought weapons they had made into the showers, and it was a perfect opportunity for multiple youths to beat up one youth.

I saw other youth being hit and choked while in the shower and had to keep my mouth shut to avoid being on the receiving end the next time. I felt extremely vulnerable and unsafe during that time of day and got out of the showers as fast as I could!

Looking Out The Window

The roof of the cell rose up at an angle outwards until it reached 15 feet high. Close to the top was a 2'x 6" rectangular window that let light into the room. If I jumped high enough, I could see a little bit of lawn and buildings through the window. I would jump and grab onto the ledge of the window and pull myself up to see out of it. It was quite the task, but I would do it when I felt extremely lonely and scared.

CHAPTER 12

YOUTH CORRECTIONAL CENTER

Age: 12
Length: 2 weeks

After two months into my second stay at the juvenile detention center, I was informed that I would soon be transferred to a Youth Correctional Center in Northern Nevada (Elko).

I was excited and nervous at the same time. I was excited because I could finally start serving my sentence. I was nervous because the facility was described by the staff and other youth as a military-style boot camp, and housed the worst youth criminals in the state.

In preparing for it, I had to have vaccines and medical tests conducted. After arriving at the nurse's office, she told me to drop my pants. When I asked her why, she told me, "So I can stick a Q-tip in your penis."

When I refused, she said that if I didn't let her do that, the guards would strap me to the table and she would be less gentle. After that, I would be locked in solitary confinement for a week. Given the two options, I decided to voluntarily let her stick the Q-tip in my penis. It was very painful and it hurt to pee for the next few days.

I felt so vulnerable and humiliated by the entire experience with the nurse. I'm not sure if the nurse was unkind to everyone or just me. Every time she had to see me, she had a sense of disgust in her voice and demeanor.

The night before the trip to Elko, I didn't get much sleep. I was filled with anxiety and fear especially since it would be the first time I was on a airplane. And I'd seen plenty of scary plane movies.

The next morning I was transferred to a different part of the facility with the five other youth who would be making the trip with me. I was instructed to change into the clothes in which I arrived at the detention center. It felt good to be back into normal clothing.

After a quick breakfast, all of us were shackled the same way as if we were going to court. However, this time we were also chained to one another. I was in the middle of two older heavy-set youth.

Then we were escorted into a van. It was much harder to walk since I was being pulled in either direction from both sides. After a twenty-minute ride, we arrived at the airport and were escorted to a seven-seat prop plane. I was in the backseat with the other two youth who I was chained to. There wasn't much room in the back and the two youth were squeezed against me. Then the pilot and guard got on the plane and the doors were closed.

The pilot started the engine which sounded like a giant lawnmower. I was quite nervous at first. After we were in the air for a bit, I got pretty excited. It was my first plane ride and I loved the view. Then, after a couple of hours in the air, we landed and were escorted off the plane. It was a bit of a struggle for the two youth to get in and out of the plane. Since I was in the middle, it was a bit of a struggle for me, too. I had no balance and was at the whim of the other two youth.

Then we got into another van and were driven to the facility. When we arrived, three guards were waiting for us. They opened the door and yelled, "Get your fucking asses out of the van."

There was no consideration for the struggles the two heaviest youth were having by navigating the seats in shackles. Once we were out of the van and released from the shackles, the yelling continued.

I was pretty hardened at that point and just started smiling at the guards while they were yelling. They told me to knock the smile off my face or they were going to smack it off of me, so I stopped.

Every youth who arrived at the facility was required to spend two weeks at the boot camp styled cottage. After we entered the building, were told to take off our clothes in the middle of the room and stand there naked until it was our turn for a shower.

I stood there humiliated for about ten minutes until it was my turn. There was no hot water or privacy in the shower. And the guards continued to yell the entire time. Then we were given underwear, socks, an orange jumpsuit, and shoes. The facility was designed for older youth so everything was too big for me. When I walked, it felt like the shoes were going to fall off my feet.

Then we were told to hurry up and read the rules which we were orally quizzed on afterward. The guards still yelled, cursed, called us names, grabbed us and yelled in our faces so their spit hit us throughout the entire quiz. When I started to cry, they yelled, "Stop fucking crying" repeatedly, but I couldn't.

That's when they told me to drop to the ground and do fifty push ups. After I did fifteen push-ups, I collapsed to the ground. They yelled at me to continue, but I couldn't. I laid on the ground crying and wanting to die!

CHAPTER 13
YOUTH REHABILITATION CENTER

Age: 12 through 13
Duration: 7 months

The Youth Rehabilitation Center was actually one of my favorite placements. It was like a summer camp compared to the two previous detention centers. While Elko only housed males, that place was co-ed. The youth were permitted to mingle at dances, movie nights and other fun events. The facility housed 100 to 150 youth in total. There was six separate buildings housing twenty-five youth in each building. Two of the cottages were for girls and the rest were for boys.

I had my own cell again and that time the cell had a desk, a metal toilet, a countertop with a sink, a cabinet, and a closet for clothes. It felt and functioned more like a room. They even kept the doors unlocked at night on most occasions. The youth in my cottage were separated into two separate groups and not allowed to talk to each other. Even though the two sides shared the building and its amenities.

The cottage looked like a big octagon in which the rooms were on the sides. The kitchen and living room were in the middle. The staffing quarters and entry point were in the front and a large bathroom and shower area were in the back. And each side had its own dining/activity area.

Staff Changes

Every afternoon, we were escorted back to our building and locked into our rooms for staff change. I didn't mind that ritual. I would lie on my bed and stare at the ceiling until my mind drifted elsewhere. Sometimes I counted the number of bricks in the ceiling. Sometimes I fell asleep. Others times, I consciously went on adventures inside my head. In that state, my woes and fears melted away, until I regained my senses and came back to reality.

After 30 minutes, a new set of guards unlocked the cells. Then all the youth met in the middle of the cottage for roll call. After everyone was accounted for, we moved onto the next activity of the day.

School

During the weekdays, most of the youth attended the school on the campus. The school functioned much like a regular school where we switched classes a few times throughout the day. Many of the youth in the facility were credit-deficient so each youth had their own work to do in each class.

Both sexes were in the classrooms at the same time. A guard in the classroom addressed all behavior problems for the teacher. A lot of flirting and note passing occurred in the classroom and hallways when the guards weren't paying attention.

Before bedtime, youth ironed their clothes to look sharp the next day. Most of the youth were allowed to have three pairs of pants, five shirts, two pairs of shoes, a sweater and a jacket. Those items were given to the facility by the youths' parents.

I arrived at the facility with one set of clothes and wore the same thing for a few weeks. I felt a bit embarrassed showing up to school wearing the same clothes every day. After the first week, I got used to it. After a few weeks, the state sent me a box of clothes.

Since a lot of the youth in the facility were in gangs, there were restrictions on what type and color of clothing could be worn. For example, no solid red, blue or green shirts could be worn. My box included two blue jean pants, khaki trousers, three white shirts, two grey shirts, socks, and underwear. I was very happy to receive the socks and underwear since I had been wearing the same ones every day.

I wasn't very social and spent most of my time listening. I learned how to talk and flirt with the girls from watching the other guys in the building who some of the girls liked. I listened to them tell each other stories about their interactions or what they were planning. Once in a while, we heard stories about guys and girls sneaking off and having sex. The guys in my building planned what they were going to do if they snuck out, but none of them went ahead with their plans.

Meals

Most meals were eaten as a group inside the cottage. Breakfast was cold cereal on the weekdays and a hot breakfast during the weekends. Lunch was sandwiches and dinner was a hot meal prepared by the staff and a few of the youth. The food was really good compared to the food at the previous detention centers.

Since we ate with silverware, after each meal, everything was counted to ensure they were all there. Once a week, a piece of silverware was missing. We were all sent to our rooms until it was found. Most of the time, it was found in the trash. When it was not in the trash, a search was conducted throughout the entire building until it was eventually found.

On the rare occasions, when it wasn't, we were locked in our rooms the entire day. We ate in our rooms and were only allowed out during school and shower time, which was especially bad if it happened on a weekend.

Commissary

There was a convenience store of sorts on campus. When some of the youth had money, they purchased snacks, books, and other items. Parents were allowed to send the youth money to purchase those things. Since I had no parents, no one sent me money. Once in a while, another youth shared his snacks with me. Every time I ate some, it reminded me of the world outside the facility.

Facility Events

On several occasions, there were events for all the youth in the facility to attend. A few events were movie nights. The side of one of the buildings was used as a screen for the projector to show the movie. Large speakers were used for the sound. Each cottage sat together on blankets on the lawn. Almost all the kids enjoyed that event.

On another occasion, many youths left the facility to attend an event in the community. I was surprised that they allowed us to leave the facility to attend an event. On a few other occasions, we went fishing, hiking, and horseback-riding.

Shower and Shaving

The facility had private showers where I felt safe and could take my time. Male youth in the facility who grew facial hair were required to shave. I hadn't reached puberty yet so I didn't need to shave. For some reason, I really wanted to shave though. I wanted to be old enough to shave and imagined myself shaving. The youth who shaved had to return the razors to the staff immediately after showering to prevent them from being used as weapons.

Youth Escape

The entry doors to the cottages remained unlocked most of the time. And on occasion, youth attempted to escape from the facility. In most cases, after a few days, the youth returned to the facility by themselves. After they returned, they were put in solitary confinement for a week. On other occasions, they were found by US marshals and brought back. There was no way I was going to try to escape. If I did, where was I going to go? That facility seemed like it was in the middle of nowhere and a long way away from Las Vegas

Braces

The Walley's paid to have braces put on my teeth, and I needed to get them serviced by the orthodontist. Three times, I was handcuffed and transported by a van to Las Vegas. The ride was a few hours each way.

I enjoyed the drive away from the facility and back to humanity. However, when I arrived at the doctor's office, I felt extremely ashamed. I had to remain in handcuffs while the doctor worked on me.

That scene must have been a first for the doctor and his assistants. They asked me questions about what I did to get arrested. I gave them short answers and just sat there crying while they looked at me with what seemed like disgust and disappointment.

A few visits later, the braces were removed and I was happy to be done with them. It took me a few days to learn how to eat and talk without them.

Trustee Status

Toward the end of their stay at the facility, the youth were given more freedom if they behaved themselves up to that point.

Being on that status granted a youth a specific set of privileges. They ate meals at the staff table which allowed them to be first in line for seconds. They were also exempt from specific chores. They didn't have to follow the same regimented schedule as the other youth. They could roam the facility at their leisure.

It felt great to have that freedom. I remember spending quite a bit of time caring for the vegetable and flower garden at the facility. The marigold flowers were my favorite!

Facility Managers

A married couple was in charge of the facility and lived in a house on the campus. I always felt a lot of love and compassion emanating from them. When they spoke at events, they sounded sincere and caring. When I was on trustee status, the wife taught me how to care for the plants and flowers in the vegetable garden.

Sad To Leave

When it was time for me to leave the facility, I became quite sad and depressed. I felt loved, safe and accepted in that facility. There were activities I enjoyed and didn't have to put up with bullying from other youth.

Since I was so sad about leaving, I started acting up and disobeying the staff. That led to them revoking my trustee status and locking me in solitary confinement for a few days.

One day I was escorted to the office of the facility managers where the husband had a chat with me. He asked me why I was acting up all of a sudden. I told him I didn't want to leave. I guess I was subconsciously acting up so they would keep me there. Even if I weren't on trustee status, it was still one of my favorite places to be in. Eventually, I was released from the facility and brought back to Las Vegas. I was scared about what was going to happen next.

CHAPTER 14
THE MEADOW GROUP HOME

Age: 13
Duration: 8 months

The next place I lived was in the Meadow Group Home. It was a specialized home for youth on probation or parole. The home was managed by an older married couple who housed five or six youth at a time.

My first month was a bit rough. Two of the youth in the home did something and I told on them. I don't remember what they did or why I told on them, but they weren't pleased and showed me the next day.

Another one of the youth in the home became sick and threw up on his blanket. The two youth I told on, took the blanket and placed it on me while I was sleeping. When I woke up I had vomit all over my face, hair, and bed. I awoke to the smell of it and rubbed it off my face. At first, I thought I was the one who threw up. Then I saw the blanket and knew what they did. I felt disgusted and humiliated.

When I told the Meadow's, the youth denied it and the Meadow's believed them and did nothing. I continued to share a room with the two youth and they continued to bully me. They made mean comments, stole my stuff, and continued messing with me while I slept. I felt scared to sleep in the home for the next month until the youth left the home. I didn't know why they left, but when they did, I felt extremely relieved.

New School

I had a hard time adjusting to the new school. I struggled to connect with "normal" youth and adults since I had just spent over a year learning how to connect with youth and adults in detention centers.

I sought out kids who looked and acted like the kids in the detention center. I didn't have much luck though. I lacked confidence, social skills and sense of self. All I wanted was to be loved and accepted.

In gym class, I wasn't allowed to participate in the activities since I didn't have gym clothes. I was waiting for the state to give me the money to purchase them. Eventually, I started to fail the class because I wasn't participating in enough activities. After the state found out, they gave me the money to purchase the gym clothes and I was finally able to participate in the class activities.

At lunchtime, since I didn't have any friends, I sat by myself to eat. I felt so depressed, lonely and ashamed that I eventually, just skipped the lunch room all together.

Other students skipped lunch as well. They went out to smoke cigarettes and use drugs. Since I didn't smoke cigarettes, I taught myself how. I stole packs of cigarettes from the supermarket and practiced smoking on the way to and from school. I also did it because I thought it made me look cooler.

Somehow, word got around to the school that I was a sex offender. In one of my classes, a girl called me a child molester and I called her a bitch. She stood up, walked over to me, and told me she was going to beat my ass. She was tall and heavy set and I was quite nervous she might succeed.

When she pushed me, I wrapped my arms around her and put her in a headlock. After a few minutes, she bit the inside of my wrist and I let her go. She took a chunk out of my arm and it was bleeding. The teacher broke it up and we were escorted to the principal's office. I was kicked out for a week.

Since I was on parole, that incident was a violation that could potentially put me back in detention. I explained what happened to my parole officer and she understood. She said it was a warning and not to let it happen again. I agreed!

When I went back to school, I was scorned by the other students. I felt so lonely and like an outcast. My other option was getting locked back up and sent to Elko. Considering the choices, staying there was a better option. So I just did what I was good at doing. I closed myself down to the outside world and focused on getting through the day. I became very good at avoidance.

Stealing Deodorant

One day at school, someone made a comment about how bad I smelled and needed deodorant. Since I was out of money, I went to the store, took a stick of deodorant, and walked out. As I was leaving, I was stopped by an undercover security officer and was escorted to the back of the store. I was asked to empty my pockets, which I did.

When I was asked why I was stealing, I explained that I had no money and that kids at school told me I smelled. I started crying and told them I was on parole and would be sent back to detention if I got arrested. They let me go and told me not to come back to the store and if I did, I would be arrested. As they escorted me out of the store I felt humbled and relieved. I continued to thank them for letting me go. As I walked home I kept thinking about how lucky I was. Especially since I'd been stealing from the store for months!

Sex Offender Counseling

I was required by the court to attend weekly sex offender counseling. A group of ten youth were in my group which met every week for two hours. We started each session by going around the room and sharing who we hurt and how we hurt them. Then we talked about our week and had a discussion about a certain topic. We also had homework to complete which was in a workbook we took home and turned in. To graduate from the program, we had to complete three of the workbooks.

The questions in the workbook asked me to describe how I felt or thought or how the youth I hurt felt during those incidents. I usually wrote one or two sentences, just enough to complete the section. I didn't have a lot of time to complete the homework since I hid it from the other youth. I pulled it out of hiding just enough to write something down and hid it again until the next counseling session. The less people that new my secret, the better!

Looking back, I'm super grateful for that counseling service even though I hated it at the time. It taught me empathy and provided me with an avenue to discuss the challenges I was facing in life at the time.

Fishing

After school and on the weekends, I rode a bike I stole to Lorenzi Park a few miles from the house. It was my place of solace where I could escape my woes. I spent hours just sitting there, watching the animals and the people. I watched people catch fish and talked to them about their experiences.

One day, I stole a fishing rod and tackle box from someone who left them there unattended. After I got home that day, I made some physical changes to the fishing pole so it was unrecognizable and then put the fishing gear in a different container.

After that, I took the equipment to the park every day. I didn't really know how to fish, so I asked others who were fishing for tips and techniques. When I caught my first fish, I was filled with excitement and a sense of accomplishment. I continued to steal fishing gear from people who had left their equipment unattended. Eventually, I had two fishing rods, a wide assortment of fishing gear, and an ability to catch fish!

Smoking Cannabis

Most of the youth in the house smoked cannabis. They excitedly gathered together and would sneak off to partake in the daily ritual. They invited me on several occasions, but I turned them down. I'd never smoked cannabis before and I didn't like the way it smelled.

One day, I joined them for the adventure and decided to give it a try. When I gave it a shot, I started coughing violently. I still didn't feel anything. They said some people don't get high on the first try. I tried it again and felt different. However, I got super paranoid and felt really weird. I passed on future offers.

Home Closing Down

One day, the Meadows informed us that they would be selling the house and all the youth would be moving at the end of the month. I was so used to moving at that point, it didn't affect me much. I was still closed down to the world emotionally and never really felt close to the Meadows anyhow. I never felt like they stuck up for me when the other youth were bullying me. I also still felt super isolated and rejected at school. So I was quite happy to leave.

CHAPTER 15
THE WADNER FAMILY

Age: 14
Duration: 3 months

The Wadners were a married couple who had a young daughter of their own. As soon as I got there, they made a point of telling me that I was never allowed to be alone with their daughter due to my status as a sex-offender.

The husband was pretty loving, kind and compassionate towards me. It seemed like his wife went out of her way to demean and demoralize me whenever she could.

She watched and judged my every move. Whenever we went out in public, she made sure I was always by her side. She introduced me as her foster kid like I was a puppy dog. She told them I was a criminal and a sex offender. If we went somewhere where there were young children, she told the other adults that I was a sex offender and to make sure they kept their children away from me.

I felt so lonely, humiliated, rejected and upset when that occurred. I didn't know how to express my frustration except to defy the orders she gave me. When I did, she responded with more consequences and isolation.

She told another youth who lived at the house and the rest of the family not to talk to me. One night, she made a nice dinner for the family and told me I wasn't allowed to eat it with them. She made a peanut butter and jelly sandwich for me and told me to eat it in the living room. And I would continue to eat alone until I was ready to respect her and become part of the family again.

On another occasion, she gave me extra chores to do because I refused to look at her while she was lecturing me. I refused to do them. So she took the family out for ice cream and made me sit in the back of the van and watch them eat the ice cream as punishment.

When things like that didn't change my behavior, she threatened to call my parole officer and have me thrown back in jail. My parole officer told me that if I got kicked out of the house, I would be locked up in Elko until I was 18 years old. Her husband tried to intervene on a few occasions so that she lightened up on me. When he did that, she lashed out at him, so he stopped. I felt so trapped and isolated.

Clothes Shopping

Once a year, the state sent me a check for $100 to buy new clothes. My clothing options were pretty slim so I was excited to get new clothes. Once I received the check and cashed it, Mrs. Wadner took me to a clothing store.

Initially she let me pick out my own clothes. Baggy clothes were one of the top trends at the time, so I picked out two pairs of baggy pants and a few baggy shirts. When I brought them to her, she had me try them on. When I walked out of the dressing room, she was appalled and said she would never take me out in public in those clothes.

Then she told me to sit down and she would pick out my clothes. When I told her that it was my money and I wouldn't allow that, she said fine. She grabbed her purse and we immediately left the store. On the ride home she told me to give her the money. I said no and then she pulled the minivan over to the side of the road and stopped. She said that we were going to sit there until I gave her the money. And if ten-minutes went by, she was going to call my parole officer. Eventually, I handed over the money.

The next day she went shopping without me and bought a pair of jeans, khaki pants, and some button-up shirts. They were very tight and not stylish. Out of defiance, I took the clothes she had purchased and threw them in the trash. That infuriated her, so she called my parole officer. After a few minutes, she said that she had told my parole officer about what I had done at the store.

The officer asked me why I was acting up when I knew I would go back to Elko if I were kicked out. I told her that I didn't care and would rather go back to Elko then continue to live with the Wadner's. She asked me why I felt that way. I told her about the way Mrs. Wadner was treating me.

She apologized and said that she had no idea that Mrs. Wadner was treating me that way and that she would come out to the home for a visit. When she did, Mrs. Wadner denied everything and bribed the other youth in the home to tell my parole officer that I was lying. The officer sided with Mrs. Wadner and told me that was my last warning.

The wife lectured and scolded me about making up lies about her. She said that she opened her home up to me when no one else wanted me and that I should be grateful for everything she did for me. She said she was disgusted with me and planned to have me thrown out if I disrespected her one more time. I felt so angry, trapped and helpless.

Sunset Park

On the weekends, the wife took me and the other kids in the house to the park. She sat in the van and watched us play the first few times. Eventually, she felt comfortable enough to drop us off in the morning and pick us up at night. On one occasion, we walked up to a man named Carlos and started talking to him. We saw him catch a big fish and we were excited to look at it and possibly touch it. He put a string into the fishes mouth and put it back in the water. The fish was still alive and could only swim a few feet before it reached the limit of the string. We laid on the ledge of the pond and watched the fish swim around for about twenty-minutes. Then Carlos started asking us questions about our life, we told him we lived in a foster home with a mean mother. We saw Carlos a few more times and stopped to chat with him every time we saw him at the park.

One day, he asked us if we were hungry. After a bit of talking, we got into his car and he took us to the convenience store around the corner. When we got back to the park, he gave us his phone number, some quarters and told us to call him anytime we wanted to hangout. The next time we went to the park, we gave him a call. He showed up with his fishing equipment and let us use it to go fishing.

Tug-of-War With Poodle

The family had a small white poodle. During those moments when I was feeling bullied and isolated by Mrs. Wadner, I retreated to the unconditional love of their dog.

One evening, the wife isolated me from the family again. When she tried to get the dog away from me, I wouldn't let it go. When I hugged the dog tightly, she grabbed the dog by the back legs as I held onto the front legs.

We pulled on the dog from opposite ends until the dog started yapping and bit me. When I let it go, she started yelling that she had enough of me and wanted me out of her home.

She immediately called the after hours number for my parole officer. She told the person who answered the phone that I abused her dog and she wanted me out of her home. The person told her that they would send someone over in the morning and if anything else happened to call 911. When she came back into my room, she said they were going to pick me up in the morning and take me back to jail. I wasn't allowed to leave the room and no one was allowed to talk or interact with me.

I laid on my bed feeling so sad, lonely and frustrated. I closed my eyes and tried to contemplate the situation I was in. At a minimum, I would be going back to juvenile detention in the morning. Most likely, I would end up in Elko until I was eighteen.

Carlos popped into my head. I remembered that I had his phone number in my wallet. I could call him with the few quarters I had. I wondered if he would let me stay with him. There was only one way to find out. I needed to call him.

I emptied out my backpack and started to fill it with clothes. When Mrs. Wadner asked me what I was doing, I said I was running away. She stood in the doorway of the bedroom and said she wasn't going to let me run away. Because I deserved to be in jail.

I just ignored her and continued stuffing as many clothes as I could in the backpack. She was a rather heavy set woman and blocked the door quite well. However, I just pushed my way through one of the sides.

As I was about to get through, she grabbed my arm very hard and dug her nails into my arm. It hurt really bad and I punched her in the nose. She immediately started to yell and cry. As I went into the bathroom to get my toothbrush and other things, she called 911 and told them I just assaulted her.

After I got my supplies from the bathroom, I put the backpack on my shoulders and headed for the front door. She told me that she had the police on the phone and that she wasn't allowing me to leave until they got there.

I told her to get out of the way. When she said she wouldn't, I asked her to get out of the way again. She still refused. So I grabbed her with all the strength I had and pushed her to the side.

After I walked out the door, I immediately started running down the street. A few minutes later, Mrs. Wadner pulled up in her minivan and continued yelling that I was going to jail for assaulting her. I ran across the street, dodging traffic and continuing to run down different streets until she could no longer find me.

After I felt that she was no longer chasing me and was out of my life, I sighed with relief. I felt calmness coming over me. A sense of freedom surged through my body. I felt nervous and excited at the same time.

CHAPTER 16
RUNNING AWAY

Age: 14
Duration: 5 days

Since Mrs. Wadner called the police and my parole officer, I was sure they were both looking for me. And if they found me, I would be arrested immediately. I needed to stay low key and avoid any interaction with the police at all costs.

I went to the payphone at a supermarket and gave Carlos a call. There was no answer. I left a message letting him know what happened, that I needed help and the number of the payphone to call me back on. I sat on the ledge next to the payphone and waited for him to call me while staying vigilant about the police and the minivan.

Twenty minutes later, the phone rang. I picked it up. It was Carlos. He asked me what happened. I gave him a full description of the day's events and asked if I could stay with him. He said I might be able to, but he would need to check with his roommate first.

He instructed me to call him back later in the evening after his roommate got home from work. I told him Mrs. Wadner was still looking for me and I wasn't sure if I could make it until then. He suggested I hide out at the park where we met and call him later from there.

After I agreed, I walked down the back streets and alleyways to avoid the police until I reached the park. When I saw a police car, I hid behind a bush until it passed. My body was full of adrenaline and I was more excited than I was scared. My life was finally under my control.

I hid in areas of the park where I had a great view of foot and vehicle traffic until it was time to call Carlos back. I saw the Wadner's van driving around the park a few times, but I was hidden quite well. I kept my eye on the minivan each time until it left.

Around 6:00 pm, I gave Carlos a call. His roommate said I could stay there for the night. After agreeing to a meeting place, thirty minutes later, Carlos came and I jumped into his car. I had an instant feeling of being safe from the police and Mrs. Wadner. For the rest of the evening, I chatted with Carlos and his roommate about my life and what happened that day.

Carlos asked his roommate if I could stay for a week. He said I could spend the night that night and we would discuss how long I could stay the next day. When they went to bed, I laid on the couch in the living room filled with gratitude for them letting me stay the night. I replayed the day's events in my head and thought about how relieved I was to be out of the Wadner's home and that I didn't have to sleep on the street.

The next day, I hung out with Carlos. Our first stop was lunch at Carlo's mother's apartment across the street. His mom didn't speak much English so I had a conversation with her through Carlos's translation. She was super nice and the food she made was yummy.

After lunch, it was time to leave. Carlos forgot his car keys and asked me to go back to his apartment to get them. When I arrived, I noticed a picture of Carlos and his roommate hanging on the wall. Carlos was standing in the front and the roommate was standing behind him with his arms wrapped around him.

As I looked for the keys, I noticed some VHS tapes with men having sex with each other on the cover. I looked at the picture again and thought to myself, "Are they gay in a curious manner?" I had only met one gay person before. He was a brother of a previous foster mom who was really nice and fun. A few minutes later, I went back to Carlos's mom's apartment.

We said thanks, goodbye, and headed out the door. After a few minutes in the car, I turned to Carlos and asked him if he was gay. He said, "Yes. You didn't know that?"

I said I didn't. When I asked if he and his roommate were a couple, he said they were. When he wanted to know why I asked him that, I told him the picture on the wall sparked my curiosity. The conversation ended there and we continued on with our day.

Later that night, the roommate said he wasn't comfortable with me staying much longer after talking to his brother. His brother said the two were breaking the law by allowing me to stay with them. In the state of Nevada, it was a criminal offense to assist a runaway.

The next day was quite similar to the previous one. We had lunch across the street and went on errands afterward. Carlos said he was going to nightclub that night and asked if I wanted to go. He said he was friends with the doormen and could get me in. I excitedly said yes.

He said I needed to wear some clothes that made me look a bit older. After we returned to the apartment, he searched through his wardrobe and had me try a few things on. I remember how nice the clothes felt and looked and was excited to be going to a nightclub.

On the way to the nightclub, he stopped at the store to purchase some alcohol. He asked me if I ever drank before. I said I tried it once but didn't like it. I tried some beer at a foster home one time and it made me throw up.

We arrived at the nightclub, parked the car and walked towards the door. Carlos talked to the doorman for a few minutes and then we walked in. The number of people and the music was a bit overwhelming at first. I followed Carlos around as he talked and introduced me to people. Many of them were surprised when they learned I was only thirteen years old.

Most of the night, I just stood there quietly and observed the people and the environment. An hour or so later, Carlos, I and a friend of his left the club and sat in his car in the parking lot. Carlos sat in the driver seat, his friend sat in the passenger seat and I sat in the back. Carlos and his friend chatted and laughed. Since they were speaking Spanish, I didn't understand a word of it. I felt the joy and excitement in their voices and had a smile on my face.

Carlos's friend was a guy who dressed and looked like a girl. I sat in the back a bit confused and intrigued by his friend. After a few minutes in the car, Carlos brought out the alcohol he bought from the store earlier and handed me one. I refused at first and then he encouraged me to give it a try. It tasted weird but was a lot better than the beer I had before.

They started asking me questions about sex. Then Carlos started rubbing his hand on my leg. After a few seconds, he started rubbing my penis. It made me uncomfortable, so I pushed his hand off my leg. When he did it again, I pushed it away again. That time, he told me to stop pushing his hand away and drink more liquor. As

I drank some more, his friend started to rub on my leg as well.

Then his friend asked, "Will you let me suck your dick and then fuck me?" I was a bit confused by that and looked at Carlos. Then Carlos and his friend talked a bit more in Spanish. I heard Carlos say $50, and his friend acted shocked. Carlos then told me his friend would pay me $50 if I agreed to do what he asked.

I told him I wouldn't. Then Carlos reminded me that I was going to need the money for food and other things and that he couldn't keep giving me food and a place forever. So I agreed to it.

As they continued talking, they rubbed my leg and penis through my jeans. A few minutes later, I started to feel sick and threw up in the back of the car. His friend got out and Carlos drove us back to his apartment.

The next morning Carlos and his roommate got into an argument. The roommate was upset at Carlos for giving me alcohol. He said that they were already breaking the law by having me stay there. He told Carlos that I needed to leave.

I no longer felt safe with Carlos or welcome in his house. I called my parole officer and told her I was turning myself in. She asked me where I was and what happened at the Wadner's. I told her everything (except the events from the previous night.) She thanked me for calling her and was glad I was safe. She understood why I ran away and wasn't upset. She said she wouldn't send me back to jail. She needed some time to find a new place for me to stay and asked me to call her back in a few hours.

When I did, she said she found me a new home and to meet up with my new foster family that night. Later that evening, Carlos drove me to a community center across town. When we arrived, I thanked him for letting me stay with him and we said our goodbyes.

CHAPTER 17

THE ELLIS HOME

Age: 13 through 14
Duration: 1 year and 2 months

When I arrived at the community center, a festive event was in progress. There were fifty to one-hundred adults and children present. I had no idea what the Ellis's looked like. So I asked around until I was pointed toward them. Mrs. Ellis, a young lady and a young man were sitting at a table talking.

When I walked up to them, I asked if they were the Ellis's. They said yes and introductions followed. After we talked for a few minutes, I set my backpack down and went to play with some other youth I had recognized at the event.

After the party ended we got into an old brown station wagon and headed to the supermarket. Mrs. Ellis was extremely overweight and it was hard for her to walk. So she used a motorized cart provided by the store to get around. Justin pushed a shopping cart behind her and his friend and I walked behind him. The two of them were very warm and welcoming. They asked me questions about my life and shared stories about the new town I would be moving to.

I felt a bit embarrassed to be walking around the store following Mrs. Ellis in her cart, but the other two were having fun and didn't seem embarrassed by it so I went along with it. Mrs. Ellis asked me about my favorite food and instructed me to pick out two boxes of cereal to eat for breakfast. We paid for the groceries, packed them safely in the station wagon and headed to my new home. Justin's friend and I flirted in the back seat during the forty-five minute ride. Eventually, she laid her head on my shoulder and fell asleep. I had a really good feeling about the new place.

When we arrived at the house, I was greeted by the family dogs and shown to my room. Afterwards I chatted with Mrs. Ellis about the rules of the house and other information I needed to know. Then I headed off to bed.

So far, I felt pretty good about the place and people. I felt really glad that I had decided to run away from the Wadners.

New School, New Start

A few days later, Mrs. Ellis drove us to the junior high school to register for classes. The town I know lived in only had one junior high and one high school. Mrs. Ellis parked the station wagon in a handicapped spot. We got out and slowly walked into the school. I felt embarrassed to be seen with her and the car as I entered the school. So I just kept my eyes down as students walked by hoping she would walk faster.

The school was not able to enroll me. They needed to receive all of my transcripts from the middle schools I had attended previously. A few weeks later, everything was sorted out and I was allowed to attend school.

My first few weeks went quite well. Many of the students came up and talked to me. They asked me to hang out with them at lunch and during breaks. They asked me about my life in Las Vegas. I told them all the stories of crime and rebelliousness that I had gathered over the past few years. They seemed impressed, and I was feeling loved and accepted.

One day a girl walked up to me and asked me if I was attracted to her friend. Her friend and I made eye contact and we smiled at each other during lunch and breaks. I was definitely attracted to her. I tried to play it cool like I learned from the other guys, and I told her friend that I wasn't interested.

A few days later, another girl came up and confronted me about why I said no to her friend. The girl was being quite aggressive and started calling me gay and other names in front of other students. I felt really scared and nervous in that moment. I really liked the girl and was upset at myself for lying and screwing it up. The only thing I knew to do in that moment was to be aggressive back.

So I started to raise my voice and she began calling me names. A few minutes later, a teacher intervened and we were sent to the principal's office. As we sat in chairs across from each other, she continued to call me names and I just sat there with me head down as tears ran down my eyes. The school had a zero-tolerance policy which meant that any disturbance at the school resulted in being suspended.

A week later I went back to school and that time I was an outcast. They called me names throughout the day and I was off to eating lunch by myself again. On the bus ride to and from school, I had to sit in the first few seats to keep the kids from bullying me. My feelings of being loved and accepted quickly had vanished. I was feeling lonely and rejected again.

At that point, I did the only thing I knew how to do. I closed down to everyone emotionally and isolated myself. During school, I just kept to myself and ignored the bullying from the other kids. At home, I spent most of my time in my room by myself. Then Quinn moved in.

Roommate Quinn

Quinn was a grandson of the Ellis who had recently been in legal trouble. The judge allowed him to stay with his grandmother instead of going to juvenile correctional center. We shared a room together and bonded quite fast. Since he was a year older than me, he attended the high school while I attended the junior high school.

We rode the bus to and from school together. Quinn made friends quite easily. I was impressed by his confidence and social skills. A few weeks after riding the bus together, I no longer needed to sit up in the front. After school and on the weekends, I hung out with Quinn and his friends. I was no longer feeling like an outcast. I was extremely thankful to have Quinn in the house with me.

Sneaking Out At Night

After the Ellis's went to sleep, they rarely came out of their bedroom. So Quinn and I would sneak out the bedroom window and went out on adventures. We stuffed our beds to make it look like we were under the sheets. Then we caught a taxi to the person's house we were going to visit. Most of the time, it was a lady Quinn was interested in.

One time we we got caught. When we arrived back to the house, we looked into the bedroom window and noticed someone had checked our beds to see if we there.

We also noticed the lights on in the living room. We knew we were busted. So we decided to walk in through the front door and grab the situation by the horns.

Quinn received bad news that day, so we decided to use it as an excuse for sneaking out. We told Mrs. Ellis that he was extremely upset and that we went out for a long walk to blow off steam. She asked if we were out drinking and doing drugs. We were, but we told her know. She said she didn't believe us.

She then asked us to walk up to the couch where she was sitting so she could smell or breaths. She didn't smell anything thanks to the breath mints we ate ten-minutes earlier on the taxi ride home. She gave us the benefit of the doubt and off to bed we went. I laid there feeling extremely proud of my ability to lie and manipulate.

Drugs and Alcohol

There wasn't much for the youth to do in this town. So the kids usually hung out at each other's houses or met up in remote parts of the town to drink, do drugs, or have sex. My social skills were still limited and I didn't have the courage to ask any of the girls out. So I didn't engage in the sex part, but I actively engaged in drugs and alcohol.

Street Gang

One night, I convinced Quinn to start our own street gang. I learned a lot about gangs while I was locked up so I felt like I knew what to do. We came up with the name "Small Town Hustlers (STH)" and we recruited two of our other friends to join us.

The first thing we needed to do was jump each other in. This meant each one of us had to stand in the middle of a circle and allow the others to punch and kick us. We went to the store, got some alcohol and proceeded to create our gang.

There were two rules. No punching in the face, and if someone fell to the ground, the clock stopped and they had to get back up and continue. I volunteered to go first and then we all took our turns. We were so intoxicated at the time that it didn't hurt that much. However, the next day all of us were pretty sore. No one really took it as seriously as I did. I started to do graffiti and gave myself a tattoo on my hand by using a sewing needle and pen ink.

Hot Tub Party

The Ellis's youngest son, Jacey, lived on his own and would occasionally stop by. Quinn and I really liked him because he was in his twenties and bought cigarettes for us. He also drank liquor and smoked cannabis with us.

On one occasion, he had some friends over to use the Hot Tub the Ellis's garage. Quinn and I hung out with him and his friends in the Hot Tub. We drank, smoked, laughed and had a good ol' time. It was a school night, so Mrs. Ellis insisted that Quinn and I head to our room at 9:00PM. At 9:30 we headed to the room while the party in the garage continued. The window in our room was near the garage door, so we could still see and hear the festivities for the next few hours.

We got ready for bed and turned the lights off as directed. Jacey knocked on our window occasionally and gave us shots of liquor and puffs of cannabis. Towards the end of the night, one of his lady friends joined him for the trip to the window.

When he knocked, she took her top off and exposed her breasts. Quinn and I quickly opened the window. After a few minutes of chatting, we helped her sneak into the room through the window. We were filled with joy to have her in our room. She was a bit loud, so we had to keep quieting her down. I let Quinn take over the talking and in a few minutes, she had her hand down our pants while we rubbed her breasts. After a few minutes, she left the room and said she would be back to get us. We waited a few hours for her to return. Eventually, we got tired and went to sleep.

An hour or so later, we heard a knock on the window. It was Jacey and his friend. We got dressed quickly, snuck out the window, got in Jacey's car and drove towards his house. Jacey's friend sat in the backseat in between Quinn and I. Once again, I remained quiet and let Quinn do the talking. Within a few minutes she was naked and had her hands down our pants. I was excited and filled with anxiety because this would be my first time with a woman.

After we arrived at Jacey's house, we had more drinks and smoked more cannabis. The lady told us she was married and not to tell anyone. We agreed and proceeded to have sex with her. During the sex, I was so nervous. Afterwards, though, I felt like a new man. The next day, we told our friends about the adventure and I was glad to finally have a cool story of my own to share with others.

Ninth Grade

The summer was over and I was really looking forward to attending school. I finally made it to high school and thanks to Quinn, I had developed a group of friends to hang out with at school. Although he was in the tenth grade, we met up at lunch and during the breaks. No longer was I friendless or bullied by the other students.

High School Football Team

Quinn and I tried out for the high school football team that summer. The tryouts consisted of two weeks of intense physical activity and training. The coaches pushed us to our physical limits every day. At the end of the two weeks, we made the team and continued to practice all the way up to the first game. On that day, the coach called us into his office. He told us that we had been cut from the team for failing classes the previous year. I was upset that I couldn't play football, but felt happy I at least made the team!

Juvenile Detention (Part 3)

One day I got into an argument with one of the other students in my class. It was a guy who had bullied me the previous year. He made a snide comment about me and I immediately got out of my seat, walked up to him and told him to say it to my face. When he stood up, the teacher intervened and we were sent to the principal's office. The town had a zero-tolerance policy at school, and youth causing a disturbance could be criminally charged.

Two officers responded. One of them was the uncle of the other student. After hearing the report from the teacher, the officer said I was at fault since I got out of my seat and walked up to the youth and started to harass him. I told him that was bullshit. He started lecturing me about cursing, so I told him to fuck off. He didn't like that very much and told me to stand up so he could arrest me. I stood up, he handcuffed me and said something "You're not such a tough guy now are you," to which I replied,

"Take these cuffs off and let's go out and see who the tough guy really is."

After a few more exchanges, it was time for him to escort me to his police car. On the way out of the building, he slammed my right shoulder into a few doorways as we walked through them. It hurt a bit and he smiled as he did it. At that point, I started unleashing all kinds of insults at him. He drove me to the police station and waited for a call back from my parole officer on what to do. During that time, we continued to trade insults. Eventually, my parole officer was on the phone talking to me. She asked me if I had done the things the officer said I did. I said yes. She told me that it was unacceptable and that I would be locked up for a month.

When she asked me to pass the phone back to the officer, she told him to send me to juvenile detention for a month and that made him quite happy. Since, there wasn't a juvenile detention in that town I had to be transported to one in Hawthorne, Nevada which was about one hour away. I had just stuck up to bullying by him and the other student, so I was feeling quite proud of myself in that moment.

Thirty days later, Mr. Ellis came to pick me up and he had a stern lecture for me. Both of the Ellis's retired from the Police Department and had very little tolerance for my actions. They stated that if anything like that happened again, I was out of the house. I agreed to behave.

Getting Kicked Out

Justin, the other youth who lived in the house, was pretty much a straight-edge kid. He got good grades, participated in school events and hung out at with his friends most of the time. So other than having dinners together, we didn't interact that much. However, one day he kicked the cat that lived with us and I started punching him for it. That was the last straw for the Ellis's. I was immediately kicked out of the house and moved over to the Casner's.

CHAPTER 18
THE CASNER FAMILY

Age: 14 through 15
Duration: 3 months

The Casner's were a married couple with a son a few years younger than me. Mrs. Casner worked as a nurse and Mr. Casner worked as a semi-truck driver. He was often gone and only home a few days out of the week. I had my own room and the Casner's were the first feeling I had of being in a normal family in a long time.

Chaos The Puppy

For Christmas that year, they let me take a dog from the shelter home. I picked out a chow puppy. He was full of energy and loved to play so I called him Chaos. I built him a fenced in play area in my room because he peed on the bed during the night. But when I put him in the play area at night, he whined really loud. At first, I gave in and let him sleep on the bed again. But then he peed and pooped in the bed. So the next night I put him in the play area and ignored his cries as long as I could.

They got louder and louder and the whole house could hear them. Mr. Casner became upset because he had to be up early the next morning and couldn't sleep. I was a bit frustrated myself.

It broke my heart a bit to listen to him cry but I didn't want to piss off Mr. Casner, so I grabbed my pillow and blanket and slept with him on the floor. He was so happy and I was happy to be snuggling with him as well.

About a month later Chaos went missing from the backyard and was never seen again. At first, I was quite heart-broken. But I got over it and didn't mind having fewer responsibilities.

Kissing Mrs. Casner

One evening, Mrs. Casner and I were in the kitchen doing dishes after dinner. Mr. Casner went to bed because he had to be up early for work. She was washing and I was rinsing. We had some music playing and were having fun with the chore.

At one point, we turned our heads toward each other and kissed on the lips. We pulled our heads back after a few seconds, looked at each other and kissed again. She was a bit shorter than me, so I picked her up and sat her down on the kitchen counter and we continued to kiss passionately.

I'm not sure what caused us to stop, but when we did, we both had big smiles on our faces and went to bed. Mr. and Mrs. Casner slept in separate bedrooms because he got up early and snored.

The next morning Mrs. Casner came into my room and woke me up. She said that Mr. Casner was gone and proceeded to kiss me. I was a bit worried that my breath didn't smell good, but she continued anyway. Our clothes came off and we had sex. We agreed not to tell anyone.

On the bus ride to school that day, I remember being filled with joy. When I saw Quinn at break time, I told him all about it. He was quite impressed. Later that night, she came into my bedroom and we had sex again.

The next day, Mr. Casner returned home. Dinner time was very interesting because Mrs. Casner and I had a secret to hide. We looked at each other occasionally and smiled. The next time occurred in the car on the way home from Las Vegas. We had sex five times in total. It felt really great to be intimate with someone and the sneakiness of it was quite thrilling as well. My whole demeanor and outlook on life improved.

Then Mr. Casner started to realize what was going on. He never caught us in the act, and Mrs. Casner insisted that she didn't tell him. But one evening after dinner, Mr. Casner had enough. He confronted Mrs. Casner in her bedroom and asked her if she was having sex with me. Their son and I could hear them scream at each other from the table

Then Mr. Casner came out and confronted me. I had a bit of a grin on my face and was a bit confrontational back to him as he questioned me. He started to get physically aggressive and I told him that I would knock him out if he placed one finger on me. That was the last straw. He called Child Protective Services and told them that he wanted me out of their house.

Mr. Ellis came and picked me up and took me back to his house. He made sure I knew that he wasn't happy about it and was only doing it because there was no other place for me to stay. I slept on their living room couch that night and Quinn was instructed not to talk to me.

The next morning, someone from the state came over to the Ellis's to drive me back to Las Vegas. First, we stopped at the Casner's to collect my belongings. When we arrived, both were at the house waiting for us. Mr. Casner was pretty irate and Mrs. Casner was crying.

As I packed my belongings, Mr. Casner came into the room and said he was taking back my Christmas gifts. They had bought me a nice stereo and a few other things. I told him that he couldn't have them and stood in front of the stereo as he went to grab it. We were in a bit of a stand-off and he motioned like he wanted to punch me, so I raised my fists and told him to bring it on and that I would knock his ass out. He yelled to the state worker that he wanted me out of his house right now and that he bought those gifts with his money so they were his.

After a few more minutes, my stuff was packed up in the car and we were on our way. During the ride, the worker questioned me about the affair. I denied everything, she didn't believe me at first and probed some more.

After twenty minutes, she stopped asking me questions. We sat silently listening to the radio for the rest of the ride. I remember feeling a sense of confidence, power, and control that I never felt before, and I liked it.

CHAPTER 19
GIRLS AND BOYS HOME

Age: 15
Duration: 2 weeks

We arrived at a large facility that was right next to a police station. I immediately started to panic because I brought my stash of cannabis with me. I pleaded with the state worker to let me smoke a cigarette before we entered. When she agreed, I walked around the side of the building, hid my cannabis in a bush, and proceeded to smoke a cigarette.

Afterwards, we walked into the building and there were children doing chores, reading, and talking to the staff. I was escorted into a private room by the state worker and a staff from the facility. After a few minutes of conversation and paperwork, the state worker was on her way. At that point, it was just me and the staff member. He explained the rules of the place. They were quite different from any other place.

The facility was a short-term shelter for youth with behavioral issues. They used a point system to attempt to alter the youths' behavior. If you did something they liked, you received positive points. If you did something they didn't like, you received negative points.

Each youth carried a point card around all day to record points. If you lost the card, you earned negative points. Each youth was required to earn so many points a day to gain basic privileges like TV and free time. To earn those points, you did chores and demonstrated what they determined to be acceptable positive behavior.

However, if you said a curse word, rolled your eyes at staff instructions, or something like that, you received negative points and were required to write them on the card. Then you had to do extra chores or assignments to earn them back or you weren't allowed to participate in the basic privileges. If you became uncooperative altogether, the staff gave you 50,000 negative points that you had to work off and you were not allowed to interact with the other youth during that time.

While I was in the room with the staff member, he asked me to empty my pockets and place everything on the table. When I refused, he said it was required of all youth as a safety precaution. After a few more minutes of discussion, I emptied my pockets on the table.

He told me the cigarettes and lighter were not allowed in the facility and took them off the table. I became a bit upset, but he attempted to calm me down and said that I wouldn't be allowed to smoke at the facility anyhow. When I let it go, he said he was going to give me 5,000 positive points for remaining calm.

He instructed me to write some things down on the card and he signed it. Then we walked out of the office and he led me to my room to unpack my belongings and instructed me to come to see him when I was done unpacking. When I returned he gave me an additional 5,000 positive points to write down on my card.

A few days later, I was instructed by my parole officer to visit her. I hadn't talked to her since everything transpired at the Casner's. The facility didn't have enough staff to transport me to see my parole officer, so I was given bus tokens and shown how to take the city bus.

As I left the facility, I retrieved the cannabis I hid in the bush and re-hid it at park down the street. After I made it to my parole officer's office, she questioned me about what took place with Mrs. Casner. I denied that anything occurred and she instructed me to not have any contact with Mrs. Casner. I agreed and the topic changed to my next placement.

She found a group home I could move to in a few weeks. After we discussed other issues, my appointment was up and I headed back to the facility. But before I did, I stopped at the park, smoked some cannabis and called Mrs. Casner to let her know how I was doing. She told me that she was sorry for everything and that she loved me. After that, I headed back to the facility. They searched me again and instructed me to write some more positive points on my card.

A few days later I was allowed to have phone calls. However, per facility rules, the person had to be approved by the guardian first, in this case, it was my parole officer. She only approved me to call Quinn.

When it was my turn to use the phone, a staff member called the approved number and waited for the person to answer. Then they asked for the approved person by name. Once the staff member believe it was the approved person, they transferred the call to another phone from which no one could make outgoing calls from. I talked to Quinn for a bit and then had him three-way Mrs. Casner so she and I could chat.

One day they found out what I was doing. I'm not sure if they overheard me or were listening to the call, but they confronted me about it. I denied it and got a bit confrontational. The staff instructed me to pull out my card so they could give me negative points. I pulled it out and proceeded to rip it up and threw it on the ground.

A few minutes later, I was at negative 50,000 points and uncooperative, as they put it. At that point, the staff no longer issued any negative points and just focused on getting the youth to follow their commands or become cooperative again.

When a youth is uncooperative, the other youth are instructed not to interact with that youth and there is a staff member at that youth's side at all times, even while sleeping and in the bathroom. I remained in that status for about two days. I did basically whatever I wanted as long as I didn't interact with the youth. I watched TV and went to the kitchen and made whatever I wanted to eat and left the dishes in the sink without cleaning them.

There was a few youth I liked talking to, so I decided to become cooperative again. The next day or so was consumed with chores and activities to make all the points back. But I did it and got to interact with my new friends again. My parole officer instructed them to allow me to leave the facility for a few hours a day. I usually went to the park down the street. I cherished that time because I could smoke cigarettes, cannabis and call Mrs. Casner.

One day, after returning from the park, one of the staff members smelled the cannabis on me and started to question me about it. I denied it and after a bit of disagreement, the staff member started issuing me negative points and I went uncooperative again. I flipped over a small table and it broke. At that point, they called the police and I went outside to smoke a cigarette. When I tried to come back in, the doors were locked.

So I headed over to the park and called Mrs. Casner and asked her to come for me. She said she couldn't and that she would get in trouble if she did. I got a bit upset and hung the phone up on her.

I hung out at the park until the sunset. I walked back to the facility and tested the doors. They were still locked, so I just sat outside the back of the facility. Later in the evening, one of the staff came out and talked to me. I agreed to become cooperative again and remained that way for the rest of my stay at the facility.

Chapter 20
Bobbit Group Home

Age: 15
Duration: 4 months

The next group home housed five to ten kids. It was managed by a married couple who lived in the facility. Other staff members helped them supervise the youth. During nights and on weekends, they were off duty and spent the evening in their studio apartment that was attached to the building.

Mrs. Casner

Mrs. Casner came up to see me while I was at that home. I met her at the convenience store. She still wanted to be my mother and I wanted to have sex with her. She wasn't comfortable with that and I had no desire for her to be in my life if we weren't having sex. I told her that and she cried. She still tried to contact me after that, but I usually ignored her.

Knee Surgery

While I was in gym class playing basketball. I went up for a shot and hit my kneecap on another youth's body and injured it. I fell to the floor and when I stood up, I felt my knee lock in place. I fell back to the floor in pain and the nurse's office was called. They assisted me out of the gymnasium in a wheelchair to the nurse's office.

A staff member from the home picked me up and drove me to the hospital. The doctors took x-rays and informed me that pieces of bone had slivered away from my knee cap and were lodged between muscles and tendons inside my knee which needed to be removed with surgery.

A week later, I was in surgery to have the slivers removed. After I woke up from the surgery the doctors explained that they got the most they could, but there were still pieces that made their way to the back of the knee that they were unable to remove. I was instructed to wear a brace on my knee and use crutches to walk for a few weeks. I had to avoid physical activity. I was quite embarrassed to be walking around school in a vulnerable position.

After a month, I was allowed to walk without the crutches. And a month later, I was allowed to ditch the knee brace altogether. On occasion, I would feel my knee lock up again and I wore the brace. I became a bit timid to participate in sports and other physical activities for a while after that.

Girlfriend Kim

One of the staff members had a niece named Kim who was living with her. Kim joined us for a few outings and we hit it off. I would catch the city bus for a few hours each way to visit with Kim. On a few occasions, we hung out at the staff member's house without the staff member knowing.

One day the staff member found out that I was going to her house and she was not happy about it. She confronted me about it and told me to stay away from her house and her niece. I stopped going to her house, but Kim and I stayed in touch almost every day.

Cannabis Baggies

One of the other students at the school provided me with a few bags of cannabis to sell to the other students. If I sold three, I got one for free. One day, the home went out for an event and one of the baggies fell out of my pocket and onto the floor.

No one saw it fall out, but the staff member noticed it and picked it up. All the youth denied it was theirs and we were promptly brought back to the home. All the youth were placed on restriction until someone confessed to owning the baggie. There was no way they could prove that it was me, so I remained silent.

One of the other youth planned to hang out with some friends that evening but he wasn't allowed to since the entire house was on restriction. He was quite sad and after a few minutes seeing him like that, I felt bad that he had to suffer for my actions. I went to the bathroom and flushed the other baggie of cannabis in my pocket down the toilet. I then told the staff that it was mine. My parole officer was called and she sent an officer to arrest me and transport me to juvenile detention.

CHAPTER 21
JUVENILE DETENTION *(PART 3)*

Age: 15
Duration: 2 weeks

Juvenile Detention was a bit different that time. I was older, physically bigger and more knowledgeable about how to navigate the written and unwritten rules of that environment. Since several of the same guards still worked at the detention facility, they welcomed me back.

That time I was also in for a crime which I could talk about with the other youths. Since I'd already been to the main correctional facilities, youth who were on their way to one of these facilities asked me questions about what it was like.

One of the youth inspired me to change up my story when I saw the judge. I told him that it was not my cannabis, and I said it was mine to keep the other kids from being punished. He said since it was not found on me, and I no longer admitted to it, that he was required by law to release me.

Although he ordered the courts to set me free, there was one hold up. They needed to find a new place for me to stay. A few weeks later, I was released and off to the next home.

CHAPTER 22

NEVADA YOUTH HOMES

Age: 15
Duration: 4 months

The next home was different than the rest. The facility was managed by shift workers, one or two staff members worked an eight-hour shift and then left after new staff came on their shift. I didn't spend a lot of time at the home other than to eat, shower, and sleep.

Girlfriend Kim

Kim moved back to living with her mom. I spent a lot of time at her house. She was my first girlfriend in the typical sense. We exchanged love letters and talked by phone multiple times a day.

One day, her mom's boyfriend was verbally abusive to Kim and her mom. I stepped in and told him to back off. Although he backed off, I was no longer allowed to come back to the house or see Kim again.

Summer Job

I landed a summer job through a youth workforce program. My job was to help clean and prepare a middle school for the next year. Three other youth and I reported to the school janitor. We did various tasks that he requested. Everything from painting to scraping gum off the sidewalks.

I really enjoyed the job. The youth working with me were cool and the janitor was laid back. He gave us tasks and told us to report back to him when we were done. Some tasks take hours and others took days. I was happy making money and being away from the home.

Quinn was also back in Las Vegas, so we reconnected and hung out on the weekends. Overall, life was good. Then I got news from my caseworker that she wanted to move me to a place where I could start learning to live independently and prepare to be on my own.

CHAPTER 23

NEVADA YOUTH HOMES
(CORPORATE OFFICE)

Age: 15
Duration: 3 months

The next home was managed by the same corporation and located in the back of their corporate office. The front of the building had three offices while the back of the building was under construction. A single door separated the two parts of the building. During the day, the door was open and at night it was locked. The offices in the back were converted into bedrooms. A kitchen and larger bathroom were being installed by construction workers during the day.

Five other youth lived there with me and a staff member supervised us for a few hours after the office closed. Once a week, the refrigerator and cupboards were stocked with food. We were in charge of preparing our own meals and cleaning up after ourselves.

That building was in one of the worst parts of town. I looked over my shoulder as I came and left. Police sirens could be heard throughout the night as we sleep. The place was a dump and the neighborhood was scary.

A few months later, all the youth in the building were moved. I'm not sure why, but I heard a rumor that the company didn't have the proper licensing or approval for youth to live in the back of the office.

CHAPTER 24
NEVADA YOUTH HOMES
(INDEPENDENT LIVING
CENTER)

Age: 15 through 17
Duration: 1 year and 8 months

The facility was a two-story apartment complex (owned by the same corporation) with two apartments on each level. It served as an Independent Living Facility and held ten youth at a time. Each apartment had a small living room, a full kitchen, two small bedrooms, and one bathroom. Three of the apartments were used for youth and the fourth apartment was used as an office and sleeping area for the staff.

There was a bit of a hierarchy about which apartment youth were in. Room seniority was based on merits such as working and going to school as well as on a first-come basis. I slowly moved my way up the chain until I lived in every apartment.

The bottom left apartment was the staff office and the bottom right apartment was where youth lived when they first arrived. Four-to-six youth shared that apartment. The top right apartment was for youth who had been at the facility a bit longer. Two youth shared a room in that apartment. The crown jewel was the top left apartment. Each youth had their own room and received other perks in that apartment.

The complex was in one of the worst neighborhoods in the city. The street where we lived was called, "Crack-Alley." Gangsters, drug dealers, and prostitutes roamed the streets continuously. Shootings, robberies, and other events occurred in the neighborhood on a daily basis. We were forbidden to walk or go anywhere in the neighborhood unless we were leaving our complex and headed east to the main street where we could catch the city bus.

But we didn't listen. We explored the area to the west and bought drugs and alcohol. A few of the neighborhood convenience stores sold us alcohol without checking our identification. Anytime I walked in the neighborhood, I put my hand on a knife inside my pocket the entire time. It was against the facility policy to have weapons and they would of kicked me out if they had found out I had it. But I felt restriction was better than death.

Butting Heads With Bernard

Bernard was the man overseeing the facility. He was kind and loving. And very passionate about structure and protocol. If the youth followed the rules, went to school (if enrolled), and worked (or were looking for work) he let the youth come and go as they pleased. I really enjoyed the freedom of the place and met the criteria most of the time.

There were times, however, when Bernard and I butted heads. One time he suspected me of smoking cannabis and confronted me. His assumption was correct, but I denied it. One of the facility rules was that you had to submit to random drug tests.

Since it was Friday evening, and the testing facilities were closing, Bernard told me that early Monday morning, we would go for a drug test. If youth failed a drug test, they were usually kicked out of the facility. Although I was nervous, I continued to play innocent and taunted him a bit before he left.

That weekend, I drank as much water as I could to flush out my system. One of the other youth suggested I drink a lot of cranberry juice as well. Since he said it worked for him, I gave it a shot. I drank so much fluids that weekend that I got sick of going to the bathroom.

The following Monday, I drove with Bernard down to the drug test facility twenty-minutes away. There was a bit of tension during the car ride. He said he knew I was going to fail the test because he could smell the cannabis on me that day. I continued to deny his accusations and prayed that my weekend flush worked. If not, I would be kicked out of the facility and sent back to Elko.

After we arrived at the testing facility, I was instructed to pee in a cup and give it back to the lab technician. But first I had to empty my pockets and I would not be permitted to take anything with me into the bathroom, except the clothes I was wearing. Initially, Bernard insisted that he be allowed to watch me pee in the cup. I told him I was not comfortable with that and would refuse to take the test in that case.

Eventually, he allowed me to urinate in private and we left the testing facility. I felt super nervous on the ride home. Bernard started to ask me questions about what I was going to do after I got kicked out. I continued to claim innocence and ignored him for the most part.

Then, 24 hours later, he got the results back. I had passed. When he told me, I was filled with joy. He said he wasn't sure how I passed, but he was quite sure I was high that day. I asked him for an apology after accusing me and he said he was sorry. Then I lectured him a bit for not trusting me.

We butted heads again when I got into a fight with, Nacho, one of the staff members. He worked at the facility during the late night and had only been working at the facility for a few weeks. The shift was hard to fill and Bernard really liked him.

Around nine o'clock on a school night, Nacho came into my room to tell me to turn the lights out, I told him I was working on my homework. He said I could spend fifteen more minutes and then it was, "Lights Out!"

Twenty minutes later, when he came in and saw me still doing my homework, he wasn't happy. Since I had been so engaged in my homework at that point, I didn't even realize that twenty minutes had passed.

He instructed me to put everything away and get into bed right now in a demanding tone. And that he was going to stand in my room until I was in bed with the lights out. It struck a nerve with me, so I told him to calm down in a demanding tone. That struck a nerve with him, so he commented on how ungrateful I was and that he would never allow me to stay up past bedtime again. I responded by telling him to fuck off!

Then Nacho approached me in a very aggressive manner. He started yelling at me and pushed me back onto the bed. When I immediately got back up, he tried to punch me in the face, but I dodged it. This caused him to lose his balance and fall on the bed. Then he got up and started to cock his arm back to throw another punch. That time I beat him to it and punched him in the jaw with all the strength I had. He immediately fell to the ground.

When he was on the floor, I offered a truce to stop the fighting. He got up and stormed out of the apartment and into the office.

The other boys in the apartment had gathered in the room and saw a good portion of the interaction. After Nacho left, the boys praised me and gave me high fives. I felt proud and scared at the same time!

Ten minutes later, Nacho came back into the apartment, walked into my room and handed me the phone. Bernard was on the other line and was very upset with me. Nacho told him I attacked him and Bernard wanted to tell me that he was tired of my shit and would call the police shortly to have me arrested and removed from the facility for good.

I tried to tell him my side of the story, but he didn't believe me and called the police. When the police came, they interviewed both of us. Nacho was being a bit of a hot head while I was remained calm and collected. The police also interviewed the other youth in the apartment who had sided with me. When they told him that, Nacho started yelling at the police who handcuffed him. All the youth laughed at him while they took him to the police car. I felt extremely grateful and thanked the police officers for believing me. They apologized that I had to go through that experience and would file a complaint with Child Protective Services in the morning.

One of the officers remained at the facility with us since there were no other adults present until Bernard arrived thirty minutes later. After the police officer left, he called me into his office and was very upset with me. Far more upset than I've ever seen him. After a bit of lecturing, he said he no longer wanted me in his facility. That I was causing too many problems and that he was driving me to a new home that night.

I packed up my belongings in trash bags, got into a van with him and headed to Emergency Youth Care Center. Two weeks later, Child Protective Services concluded their investigation and the I was moved back to the Independent Living Center. Gerard was not happy that he had to accept me back.

Falling Asleep In Spanish Class

On school nights, I made it home from work around midnight. I then woke up at 4:00 AM to ride the city bus for two hours so I could make it to school on time. I was able to keep myself awake in most of the classes except Spanish.

I was excited to take Spanish and I was engaged in learning it, practicing on the bus and doing homework at times. There was always more homework than I felt I could do, so I focused on the easy parts of each class. I turned in whatever I could complete, and prayed for the best.

One day, the Spanish teacher asked me to stay after class. She asked me if I liked Spanish. I told her yes. Then she asked me why I was always sleeping in her class. I told her that I wasn't getting much sleep because of my hectic schedule. She asked me to explain my schedule.

I told her after school was out, I rode the city bus for an hour to work. Then I worked an eight-hour shift and caught the city bus home for another hour around midnight. Then I woke up at 4:00 am to ride the city bus for two hours to make it to school on time.

After that day, she no longer woke me when I fell asleep in her class. A month later, the school was let out. And when I got my report card, she gave me a C even though I didn't earn it. I was filled with joy and gratitude.

Alternative HIgh School #1

During the school break, Bernard determined that riding the city bus to school each day was too hard for me and that I needed to go to a closer school. The commute was very draining on me, but I was tired of moving schools. He said I didn't have enough credits to earn my diploma in a typical four-year time frame. So I needed to go to an alternative high school which was designed to help students like me graduate. Eventually, I agreed and switched schools

Christopher Brooks

The next one was also across town but a bus picked me up and dropped me off a few blocks away from the facility. The bus ride was 45 minutes each way, compared to the two hours it took me previously.

The school bus was never more than half full so many of us were able to take an entire row of seats for ourselves. For some reason, I loved it when the bus drove on the freeway. I was amazed that the bus driver went at high speeds. I loved looking out the window and down on the cars. Sometimes people waved at us and sometimes we would initiate the wave. Either way, it brought big smiles to our faces. I was glad Bernard made me switch schools!

The school was filled with misfits like myself, so I fit right in. Many students at the school smoked cigarettes. An empty dirt lot next to the school was where the students smoked during breaks. The school allowed us to smoke as long as we didn't smoke on campus. A staff member patrolled the area on the lookout for cannabis as well as other unwanted behaviors and actions. To skirt that, students emptied out cigarettes and black, mild cigars and then filled them with cannabis, so it looked like they were smoking tobacco products.

One day, the history teacher told the class he couldn't smell anything, so students smoked cannabis at the back of the class in a bit of an ingenious way. When the teacher wrote on the board, one of the students ducked his head under the desk and took a hit of cannabis from a pipe. The

152

key was to minimize the smoke. So the student immediately put out the fire and blew the smoke very softly into a towel until it was all absorbed. Then the towel, pipe, and lighter were passed to the next person.

That is until the principal of the school walked into the room unannounced one day. She took a few steps into the room and commented that the room smelled like cannabis. The teacher said he didn't smell anything but not to depend on his opinion since his nose didn't work.

The principal asked the teacher what she needed to ask and then turned to the class and asked us if we smelled the cannabis in the room. Some of the kids responded yes. And then a student who was a know cannabis user made a joke that he needed to do his laundry. Many of the students laughed and the principal exited the classroom.

I only spent a month at the school. There was one closer to my house, but the home address in my school file was outdated and they zoned me for the wrong school. I went there until the adults figured it out.

Alternative School #2

The next school was quite similar to the previous one with an added benefit, the bus ride only took half as long. The school offered additional classes that could be taken at the end of the day to earn additional credits. A vocational high school was next to the alternative school.

It offered classes in several areas including the culinary arts. Students from the alternative school were permitted to take classes at the vocational school if there was room. Home Economics was one of my favorite subjects in school. So I was excited to learn that I could learn to be a Chef at the school.

On the first day, I was shocked to see Quinn in the class as well. He was going to a regular high school nearby, but he was also taking the class to make up lost credits from our time together at his grandma's. We were thrilled to be taking the classes together. That class had a total of seven students including Quinn and me.

The other students in the class were members of the vocational school who were quite serious about taking the class and learning from the chef instructor. Quinn and I didn't take the class as seriously and goofed off a bit as we completed our assignments. One day after class, the instructor pulled us aside and gave us a choice of taking the class seriously or being stuck on dish duty for the remainder of the semester.

We apologized and told him we would behave. However, on the next assignment we goofed off a bit as well. The next day we were assigned to dish duty. After five days of doing dishes, Quinn and I decided to quit the class.

My Friend Rick

During breaks, I hung out in the back of the alternative school in the smoking section. At this school, students were permitted to smoke cigarettes on campus in a designated area monitored by security guards. One day, during lunch, Rick, another student, asked me if I wanted to go have a hamburger with him for lunch. I told him I didn't have any money. He said he would pay for it, so I said "Yes."

The restaurant was a five-minute walk from the school. And many students made the trek each day. When I thought we were going to walk, he said he had a truck with airbags that lifted the car up and down like an amusement ride and a stereo system with ten giant speakers.

When we got in the truck, he hit a switch that lifted the body off the ground just enough to clear speed bumps. When we left the school grounds, he turned the stereo up and the bass was so intense, it hurt my ears. A few minutes later I asked him if he could it down a bit. I felt embarrassed to ask him, but I couldn't take it any longer. He turned it down, called me a pussy in a playful tone, and we laughed.

We ordered our food and drove to the airport where we watched planes take off and land as we ate our food. We had a great conversation and ended up getting back to class a bit late. Rick lived near me and offered to drive me home after school. I had extra classes and got out later, so I had to pass on his offer. However, I asked if he was willing to pick me up in the morning and he said yes. We became good friends for a few years after that.

Campus Monitor With Fancy Nails

One of the campus monitors had extremely long, natural fingernails. They were so long that they made me wonder how she wiped her butt. I thought it was ridiculous but she loved them and they were always painted nicely. She was a kind, but firm, campus monitor. Most of the kids liked and respected her.

One day, she was called to break up a fight between a few students. In the process, she broke one of her nails. She was livid. I wasn't there to watch it first hand, but news of it traveled around the school fast.

Looking back on it, I think the reason we adored that lady, was her pride in expressing her uniqueness, no matter how weird or fascinating people found it. That gave us permission to express our own uniqueness.

Dropping Out Of School

One day during class, a visitor came in the classroom and handed the teacher a piece of paper. She read it and said: "Chris, you're wanted in the office." I was a bit stunned and looked at the teacher and said, "Me?" She said, "Yes, you" and smiled.

I grabbed my backpack and walked with the visitor who was another student working in the principal's office in exchange for credits. She told me the principal wanted to see me. I asked her if she knew what it was about but she said she didn't. As we walked to the office I thought about all the rules I might have broke recently.

Ten minutes after I arrived, the principal came out to see me. The warm introduction and smile on his face threw me by surprise. We walked back to his office and sat down facing each other.

He told me I was more than a year behind in credits and that I was not a good fit for the school. I was shocked and confused. I had only failed a couple of classes and thought that's why I was going to that school, believing I could make up for the lost credits and earn my High School Diploma.

He told me I wasn't in many of the previous classes long enough to get credit for them and that's why I was credit deficient. He said he was also bringing it up because I was taking up a spot at the school which another youth could use to graduate on time.

In a kind and compassionate way, he shared my options and the best one was getting my General Education Diploma (G.E.D.). If I took a test and passed it, I wouldn't have to go to school anymore. The conversation came to a close and I excitedly caught the city bus home.

When I arrived, I told Bernard about the conversation I had with the principal. He said he couldn't take my word for it and would talk to the principal the next day. The next morning, Bernard and I drove to the principal's office and the two of them had a lengthy discussion. Eventually, Bernard told the principal that he understood his reasoning and withdrew me for the school. I walked back to Bernard's car filled with bewilderment. I still couldn't believe that I was being allowed to dropout of school.

Telemarketing

Since I was no longer going to school, I was required to get a job. I worked over six different jobs while living at that facility.

My first job was as a telemarketer selling long distance phone service. First I had to go through a week of intense training. The workplace had a strict dress code and I did not have the close for the job when I accepted the position.

When I told Bernard, he said he didn't have the money to buy those items for me, but would request money from the state. The night before my first training day, I had to barter with one of the other youth so I could use some of their dress clothes.

Three days later, Bernard received a check from the state and took me shopping for dress clothes. I went to work the next day feeling handsome and much more confident.

I worked at that job for about a month before I quit. I didn't like the feeling of bothering people and being hung up on all day. I made almost $1,000 from my short time there so I was pretty thrilled. I also had some nice clothes that I could wear for future interviews.

Fish Fry Restaurant

My next job was at a fast food restaurant that served fried fish, chicken, and other items. I really enjoyed that job and was making good money. My job was to operate the three large deep fryers. It was pretty easy, except for the cleanup. Every night I got burnt somehow, someway. Usually, it was from the hot oil splashing on my hands, arms, or face.

The manager and staff really liked me. I was friendly, worked hard, and was dependable. One of the cashiers and I flirted, even though she had a boyfriend. One day, while taking out the trash together, we kissed. I remember feeling a bit torn at that moment. I enjoyed kissing her, but we were right next to the dumpster which smelled really bad. The odor was so intense we stopped and went back inside the restaurant.

One night, she invited me to her parents' apartment where she was staying to have sex. I said yes and very much enjoyed our time together that night. The next day, she told her boyfriend and that was the end of that. We remained friends at work and flirted occasionally.

While at work one day, I received a call about one of my good friends who had just been killed. I went to my boss and told her I needed to leave immediately. It was dinner time and the restaurant was busy. She said I couldn't leave at that time. She said she was sorry to hear that he died, but needed me and that if I left, I would be fired. I went to the bathroom, changed my clothes, clocked out, handed her the uniform, and ran to the bus stop.

Basketball Arena

My next job was in a large arena for basketball games, concerts and other events. Quinn was working there and was able to get me an interview. It was a bit tricky though. A person had to be sixteen years old to work there, and I was a few months short. The interviewers liked me and made an exception to the rule and told me not to tell anyone.

I was thrilled for the new job. I worked side by side with my best friend, and I was able to see concerts and events for free. Even though I worked part-time, I earned just as much as when I was working full-time at the fish fry restaurant.

I was part of a three-person team that cooked food in the back of a food stand in the main concourse of the arena. Quinn was the lead cook and made the hamburgers. I was second in command and oversaw the fryers that cooked the chicken fingers and fries. The low man was the server in between us who put the hot food in paper trays. Every event, they rotated someone different to do the server role until our friend Matt got the job. Then it was the three amigos in the cooking section. It felt great!

Our stand closed 30 minutes before the other stands. If we cleaned up fast, we were able to watch the end of all types of concerts, sports games, and events. At the end of the night, each stand evenly distributed the tips received amongst all those who worked in the stand. Many nights we each left with $50 or more. That is until someone made a big stink that they weren't paid the right amount of tips. Then they stopped allowing tip jars in the stands.

Since I wasn't making as much money, Bernard told me I needed to get a full-time job, so that's what I did. I continued to work events in my spare time when I could. But the morale of the staff in the arena was never the same after that and eventually, all three amigos quit working there.

Chicken Roasters

My next job was at a fast food restaurant that served chicken cooked in a rotisserie oven. It was a bit boring and I was only working part-time. When I told Quinn about the job, he said that he might be able to get me an interview at the restaurant he was working at. I went in for the interview, got the job, and didn't show up for my shift at the chicken restaurant the next day.

The Steakhouse

When I arrived to work on my first day, they instructed me to wash dishes. I wasn't thrilled about that, but I smiled, said yes, and did the dishes as instructed until my shift was over.

There was a large, industrial strength dishwasher, which cleaned and dried a lot of dishes in a matter of minutes. Dishes from the customers and kitchen were placed on a long metal counter next to me. My job was to rinse the big chunks of food from the dishes with a powerful spray faucet and put them in the dishwasher for a thorough cleaning.

Every time I cleared the pile of dishes, it filled up again. At some points during my shift, the pile overflowed and someone else had to stop what they were doing to help me get caught up.

After four days of doing dishes, I was finally assigned to cook food. I was a bit slow, so they put me back on dishes. I was pretty upset, but my manager said if I didn't like it, I could leave. The next day, I decided to quit. I never called or showed up at work.

Quinn was quite upset with me. He said that he had put his name on the line by getting me the job and now I made him look bad. I apologized and shared that I went there to be a cook, not a dishwasher. He was so upset that we didn't talk for months after that.

Sandwich Shop

My next job was at a sandwich shop. I wasn't thrilled to be working there, but it was only a five-minute walk from my house and it got Bernard off my back.

The job was pretty easy. Customers came into the shop, told me or a co-worker what they wanted on their sandwich and we made it. I usually worked the evening shift, so my job also included cleaning the store and preparing food for the next day.

I only had one main challenge with that job. It was with one of my co-workers. She made sexual comments and innuendos throughout the shifts. That made me quite uncomfortable but I didn't know how to express it, so most of the time, I just ignored her.

One evening, while I was walking home from work, five men followed me home. I opened up my pocket knife and held it close to my side out of their view. When I got close to my apartment, I started running and tried to open my door. As I was about to open it, they caught up with me and beat me up.

The next thing I remember was waking up in my apartment covered in blood. Then I heard a loud knock on the door. For a few seconds, I thought it might be the same group coming back. I ignored the knocks until I heard "Police open up." I went into the kitchen, grabbed the biggest knife I could find and opened the main door with the screen door locked. It was two police officers. They asked me to put the knife down and let them in.

The next thing I remember was waking up in the hospital. I carried a piece of paper in my wallet with important names and phone numbers. Billie, the guy in charge of supervising me, was called and he showed up at the hospital to pick me up.

Later on, I found out who did that and why they did it. Rick and another guy liked the same girl, so one evening, Rick asked me to go with him to a guy's house to confront him. When we did that, Rick ended up throwing a brick through the guy's window.

That guy found out where I lived and he and a group of his friends got their revenge on me. After I learned that it was retaliation for those actions, I felt like I kind of deserved it and let it go.

My Friend Jesse

Quinn and Jesse lived in the same apartment complex and the three of us would hang out at Jesse's house or roam the Las Vegas Strip. Most of our hangout sessions included consuming alcohol, cannabis, and other drugs.

The apartment complex where they lived was full of drug dealers, so we had no problem acquiring those substances. I usually spent the night at Quinn's apartment. His mom loved me and always made sure I had food to eat. Quinn's mom and step-dad argued a lot. Since Quinn and his stepdad didn't get along very well, we spent as little time there as possible.

Matt was Jesse's friend who came over occasionally on the weekends. One day, while I was at work at the fish fry restaurant, I received a "911" message on my pager and immediately called the number displayed.

The person on the other line was crying and told me Jesse was dead. According to the police report, Jesse and some people he recently met were playing Russian roulette. That game involved putting one bullet inside a revolver pistol, spinning the revolver, and taking turns putting the pistol to your head and pulling the trigger.

When Jesse pulled the trigger, the pistol blew his brains out. I visited the garage where it occurred that night and saw the blood and brain matter on the walls. When Quinn and I questioned the other people Jesse was with that night, their stories didn't match up. Jesse was left-handed but he was shot on the right side of his head. I was devastated by losing my friend.

Quinn and I wanted to avenge our friend's death but we didn't know what to do. Everyone said he killed himself, but we felt differently and couldn't prove it, which was probably a good thing since we were ready and prepared to do serious harm to someone.

A few weeks later, Quinn and I started reflecting on our friends and the lifestyle we were living. We came to the conclusion that if we continued the path we were on, we would be dead or in jail before long.

My Friend Matt

Matt and I started hanging out regularly after that. His parents underwent a criminal background check so I could spend the night. As a ward of the state, any time you want to spend the night at someone's house, anyone over eighteen who lived in the house had to submit to a federal background check.

I was usually too embarrassed to tell my friends that when they asked me to stay the night. I just told them I was on restriction and would make up a story why. In this case, when Matt was a bit persistent, I finally told him why I couldn't spend the night. He then told his parents and they offered to do the background check so I could spend the night.

Matt's parents really liked me and I liked them. They also would let us drink and smoke cannabis at the house as long as we didn't leave. We cooked dinner, watched TV and played video games most of the time.

We started hanging out at my place more often. Matt liked watching the drug dealers and prostitutes conduct business from the safety of my living room window. It fascinated him for some reason.

The day when Matt's pregnant mom gave birth, I received a "911" message on my pager. I called back immediately. It was Matt who said his mother died while giving birth. I dropped everything and literally ran as fast as I could, two-miles down the street to the hospital he was calling from. He was never the same after that.

Crashing Billie's Car

The owner of the facility lost his license to house youth at the complex. I'm not sure why that happened, but all the youth were moved to another facility across town, except me for some reason. I was super excited to be able to stay at the facility all by myself with less supervision. A month later they moved an adult into the apartment.

Billie was given free rent in the apartment in exchange for supervising me. However, he had a regular job, and because he was a boxer he was really only home to sleep. We liked each other but only interacted a few minutes each day.

On one occasion, I asked him to teach me how to drive. I just received my driver's permit, which was quite the task. At that time in Nevada, you were allowed to get your driver's permit if you were sixteen years old, had parental permission and passed the driver's exam. I was older than sixteen and knew I would pass the test. However, the state wouldn't sign off on it for any youth. So I paid an adult to pretend he was my guardian and sign the paperwork at the DMV. It worked and I got my driver's permit.

Although I knew the laws for driving, I had very little experience in driving. I asked Billie if he would teach me. He agreed and I was excited to learn. On the second lesson, I crashed his car. I was getting onto the freeway too fast and crashed into the sidewall. He was pissed, especially since he didn't have any insurance. I felt extremely bad but was a bit confused about why he would allow me to drive without insurance. I had about $500 dollars in my bank account and gave it all to him to get a new car.

Room Searches

Bernard usually came once a week to take me food shopping and inspect the apartment for cleanliness and illegal contraband. He gave me $25 dollars a week to spend on food. I usually bought the same thing every week - cereal for breakfast, sandwiches for lunch, and spaghetti for dinner.

He also showed up randomly to check on me. He rarely came after business hours or on weekends. I had a pet hamster which I let roam around my room at night and on the weekends. It was against the facility policy to have a pet, so during the day, I hid the hamster and other illegal contraband anticipating an unexpected visit from Bernard. He didn't search very hard so it was quite easy to hide those things.

The day I was beaten up while coming home from work at the sandwich shop was my last day living at the facility.

CHAPTER 25

NEVADA YOUTH HOMES
(GROUP HOME #2)

Age: 17 through 18
Duration: 3 months

Billie drove me form the hospital to a group home across the valley which Bernard managed. I asked about my belongings and was told they would be picked up and delivered for me. I started to panic because they would find all my forbidden belongings. Two days later, my belongings arrived in black trash bags and cardboard boxes. Bernard found my hamster and cannabis paraphernalia. He wasn't happy and put me on permanent restriction. I was only allowed to leave the house to look for work and for school and had to return home immediately.

I also had to take weekly drug tests. I was bummed out about those restrictions at first, but I quickly saw the silver lining. Almost any job paying more than minimum wage required the applicant to pass a drug test.

I was about to turn eighteen, would be on my own, and needed a higher paying job to support myself. I stopped smoking cannabis and started looking for jobs in the casino industry.

Two months later, I registered for a labor union. I went to the main office every morning by 6:00 am and waited with a group of other job seekers for my name to be called. Those jobs were on a first-come, first-serve basis. Except, those who were members the longest and had experience were selected first.

After two weeks, my name was finally called. I was given the job of an on-call bus person and dishwasher inside of a casino. At first, I only worked a few days a week. Most of the time, I received a call a few hours before they needed me. When someone called in sick or didn't show up for work, that's when they called me. Since I lived across town from the casino, it usually took me an hour or more to get to work. It was quite a hassle, but I just kept telling myself that it would be worth the hassle someday.

Then one day, they needed someone to help with room service and I volunteered. My job was in assisting the room service workers to prepare orders and gather the dishes from the rooms. After that shift was over, I went back to my other position.

Two weeks later, I was offered a position to help with room service one day a week. That was added to my three days helping in the other restaurants. A month later, they offered me a job working strictly in room service four days a week. I accepted the job and was thrilled. The room service manager told me that technically she wasn't allowed to hire me due to seniority. But since she liked the way I worked, she bent the rules and made an exception.

I wasn't doing anything but working and going home, so I was able to save my money and had $1,000 in the bank. I almost had enough to buy a car, so I hired a driving company to teach me how to drive.

A few weeks later, I turned eighteen and went to court. The judge was impressed that I was working and staying out of trouble. He offered to pay me the $500 that they were paying the foster parents until I was nineteen years old, as long as I continued to work and attend school. Later that day, I headed to the DMV, signed up to take my driver's test, and received my driver's license on the first try.

A few weeks later, I put all my belongings in Quinn's car, said goodbye to Bernard, and headed off on my own. That was the first time in my life in which I felt I was completely in control of my destiny. It felt awesome, scary, and humbling at the same time.

CHAPTER 26
LIVING ON MY OWN

Age: 18

An unfurnished, 8' by 10' room with no windows was vacant at the four-bedroom house Quinn was renting from. When I arrived at the home and walked inside, I was shocked. The place was filthy. The kitchen sink and countertops were filled with dirty dishes, the floors were coated with dirt and the shower tub was coated with a black layer of grime. It wasn't exactly what I had imagined, but the rent was only $250, so I said yes.

I was finally a free adult. I no longer had to report to anyone and I could come and go as I pleased. I spent all my free time over the next few days smoking large amounts of cannabis and cleaning the house. I figured that if I wanted to live in a clean house, I was going to have to take the responsibility of cleaning it. I felt that it was a small price to pay for my newfound freedoms.

Since the state would be covering my rent for a while, I could use my savings to purchase a car. I thought it would make my life so much better. I had my mind set on a particular kind of car. I was a big fan of lowriders at that time of my life and wanted to build my own.

I gathered all the classifieds I could find and continued searching until I found the specific type of car I wanted. A month later, a used car dealership had one for $3,500. I put $1,000 down, financed the rest, and drove off the lot with my first car.

Normally, it took me an hour to get to work on the city bus, but with my new car, it took less than twenty minutes. When I went to work that night, I was feeling extra great. I had a job, my own place, and now a car. They were the three ingredients I thought were essential to becoming a successful adult.

Laid Off

A few months later, I was laid off from the casino. It was the slow season in Las Vegas and the newest hires were laid off first. I was shocked, angry, and stunned by fear. What was I going to do? Then I remembered that my rent would be paid by the state, so at least I had a place to stay. I also still had about $500 saved up, so I could make my car payment and other bills for a few months if necessary.

One of my roommates had two jobs. He was a valet attendant in the evening and delivered newspapers in the early morning. He said he might be able to get me a job delivering newspapers.

The next day, he told me his boss said they were always in need of help. I went to his office, applied and got the job. During my first few days, I drove with someone and learned the route. The job took almost five hours each night and was pretty easy.

The first few hours were spent rolling up hundreds of newspapers and putting them in individual plastic bags. I filled my car with as many newspapers as I could fit into it. Then I drove slowly down the streets on my route and tossed the papers out of the window to the houses that were supposed to receive them. It took me two carloads to complete my route.

Two months later, I got a part-time job as a cook in a local mall and I worked both jobs for a while. A month or so later, I got a full-time job working as a photographer at an airport.

Brad the Mentor

The state had a few requirements I had to maintain to continue receiving the monthly checks. One of the requirements was to meet with a mentor at least once a month. I didn't really know what a mentor was, nor did I care. If meeting with that person meant receiving a check every month, then I would do it and I treated it like a job.

During the first few months we spoke, I made sure Brad knew that I was only speaking to him because I had to. He continued to call anyway. Then, one day, he asked me to help with a study he was conducting and said he could pay me for helping. I was all ears.

He was preparing to conduct a study on what happens to foster youth in Nevada after they leave foster care. He would be sending out questionnaires to former foster youth and wanted to test the questionnaire on me. He said it would take about an hour and offered to pay me $50 or so to help.

After I answered the questionnaire, he offered me a part-time job helping him with the study. He needed someone to put the questionnaires in the envelopes, seal them, and attach the mailing address. He offered $10 an hour and said it should take about 20 hours. A week later, I called him and told him I was finished. It took about ten hours, but I told him it took twenty hours. We met up for dinner, I gave him the envelopes, he gave me the $200, and we went our separate ways.

Legislative Testimony

One day, Brad called and invited me to dinner. He had received the results of the study he conducted. They weren't good. He planned to share them with certain people and wanted to know if I was willing to share my story with a few legislators. I remember thinking, "What are legislators and why would they care about my story?"

He said he was hoping to convince those people to continue supporting foster youth financially up to the age of twenty-one and he felt that my story would help. I thought about it for a few moments, especially the part where I would continue receiving a check from the state until I was twenty-one years old. I looked at him, smiled, and said I was in.

We met for dinner a few more times over the next month. Brad helped me write my story down on paper so I could read it out loud at the legislative hearing. Early one morning, I put on the clothes I used for job interviews and headed to the hearing across town.

I arrived at the large building, went through the metal detectors, and headed to the room where I was instructed to meet Brad. Since there was a construction project in the building, I got lost and asked one of the security guards for help in escorting me to the room.

When I arrived, there were a handful of people in the room. Some were sitting and others were standing. When everyone seemed serious, I started getting nervous. When I saw Brad sitting in one of the rows, I started to feel better.

I walked toward him, said hello, and sat down. He introduced me to the person sitting next to him and the three of us started chatting. Ten minutes later, the room had filled with people and the legislators sat down in really fancy chairs positioned above us. It was similar to the way the judge sat above people in court.

Presenters took turns talking to those people for 45 minutes. Then it was my turn. One of them called me up. They also called up a girl who also grew up in foster care. When I went to the stand, at first, I nervously read aloud what I had written on paper. Then the legislators asked me a few questions and it became the girl's turn. She was around my age and shared her story. Then they asked us more questions about our experiences growing up in foster care. I don't remember the questions, but I do remember one of my responses. I asked how many of those people had kids who were over eighteen years old. A few of them raised their hands. Then I asked how many of their kids were ready to be on their own at the age of eighteen.

They looked at each other and paused for a few moments. Then, one of them said he had a 23- year old daughter who just moved back home. Then another person said he had a 20-year old son who hadn't left the house yet.

Then I said, "Exactly. Your kids aren't ready to be on their own and you are good parents. How can you expect teens who have grown up in foster care to be ready to be on our own at eighteen?"

They looked at each other and then thanked us for sharing our stories. After a few more presenters, the hearing came to a close.

After the hearing, someone from the newspaper approached me and asked me questions. Then a few of the legislators came up to me and congratulated me on a job well done. One also asked me if I ever thought about being a politician. I didn't know what that meant and just laughed it off.

I left the building feeling confident, inspired and heard. As Brad walked me to my car, I asked him when he would find out if they would continue supporting us financially. He said very candidly that he had no clue and was not positive they would say yes.

My Nineteenth Birthday

On October 4th, 2000, I went before the judge for the last time. The state still had not passed any legislation that would allow foster youth to stay in care after nineteen years of age.

It was time for them to release custody of me. The judge, my caseworker, and other state officials wished me the best and I was on my way. It was a bittersweet moment. I was happy to be free from the state's care but was also losing the $500 they sent me every month to help cover the bills. Now I was really on my own and it felt scary.

A few weeks later, I called my old caseworker and asked if I could see the files they had collected on me since I was a kid. I was interested in finding my biological family and there might be clues in the files that could help me.

She said she would put in a request and let me know when she received them. A week later she called to inform me that two of the three files were missing, but that she had one of them. She left it with the receptionist for me to view whenever I was ready.

When I arrived, the receptionist escorted me to a private room and placed the heavy file on a table in the room. Then said I could use the copier if I wanted to make copies of anything. As she left the room, she told me to bring the file back to her when I was done.

I was upset that they had lost two of the files, but I was happy they had at least one. The one they had contained the court reports from the day I entered foster care and an old picture of my mom. It was the first time I ever saw what she looked like. I started reading a few pages and became overwhelmed with sadness and anger. I couldn't continue reading at that time.

Since I had to be at work soon, I decided to just take the file and walk out the door. Partly because I felt they no longer had a use for it and partly because I didn't trust them to keep the file safe.

My caseworker called me the next day to ask if I got everything I needed from the file and I said yes. She asked me where I left it, and I told her I stole the file. She wasn't happy about that but said she understood why I took it. She wished me well and asked me to call her occasionally to let her know how I was doing.

National Foster Youth Council

After I was released from state custody, I wanted nothing to do with anyone from the state, including Brad. He kept trying, so eventually, I called him back.

He said he had a great opportunity for me and wanted to know if I would meet him for dinner. He wanted me to apply for a position on the National Foster Youth Council and brought along the application. The Council was comprised of twenty to thirty foster youth from around the country who were involved in Child Welfare Reform. Brad thought it would be a great opportunity and assisted me in completing the application.

A few weeks later, I received a call from the organizer of the group. After a lengthy phone interview, she informed me that I had been selected to join the group. I was thrilled, especially since they paid the youth to attend the gatherings. The Council met twice a year, once in

Washington D.C. and another city was chosen by the group of youth.

Three months later, it was time for me to attend my first meeting. I packed my suitcase and boarded a plane to Washington D.C. I was excited and nervous at the same time. This was my first time on a big plane and my first time in Washington D.C.

The group provided us with money beforehand to take a taxi to the hotel. I wanted to save money, so I took the subway instead. I got off at the wrong stop and I felt lost, scared and confused. I ended up walking two miles in the light rain until I arrived at the hotel and thought to myself, "The next time, I'm taking the taxi. Screw the money!" Then I walked up to the front desk to check in. I was wet and exhausted from carrying my luggage.

I had arrived too early so my room wasn't ready for a few more hours. I was frustrated, scared, and had nowhere else to go. The woman at the front desk suggested that I go into the bathroom and change my clothes and that I could wait in the hotel lobby until my room was ready. I did that and an hour or so later, she informed me that my room was ready.

When I entered the room, I was shocked by how beautiful it was. There was artwork on the walls and the bed was the most comfortable bed I had laid on in my life. There were multiple faucets in the shower, including one on the ceiling which mimicked rain. I was filled with joy as I took a shower and totally forgot the challenges I faced that day.

Then it was time for dinner. The restaurants in the hotel were too expensive, so I wandered the neighborhood looking for fast food. I found a restaurant, got my food, and headed back to the hotel.

The next day, the group met at nine o'clock in the morning. I was thrilled to interact with other foster youth from across the country and listen to their stories. Most of the youth already knew each other and only a few of us were new to the group.

I met with the group three more times over the next two years. We developed instruction guides for foster youth which included how to find and obtain housing and a travel guide informing youth about the intricacies of traveling. We shared our stories and policy recommendations with politicians, high-level government employees, and the media. I developed a bond with those youth like I'd never felt before. I left feeling inspired and filled with joy each time I attended the council.

Step Up Program

A few years after I testified before the state legislator, they passed a new law known as AB94. That law added an additional dollar in taxes to business licenses filed in the

State of Nevada. That money would be used to support foster youth after they existed care.

Although I was too old to receive any of that money, a group was formed to decide how to spend it. Brad notified me about the group and said they were looking for a former foster youth to be in the group and recommended that I apply. I applied and got the position.

We met once a month and discussed the best ways to distribute the money to the youth. There were over one million dollars in the fund. We were told that we had to start using it or the money would be taken away and used elsewhere. We provided each youth who had applied for the program up to $7,500 dollars a year to be used for paying their rent, cars, job training, etc.

A year into the program, a few of us on the committee became concerned about setting those youth up for failure. Essentially, we were giving them good fishing poles, but we didn't provide them with instructions about how to catch fish.

Many youths were still unemployed or homeless. After they used up their funds, we decided to hire a mentor to assist the youth in finding jobs, housing, etc. Almost all the money in that fund went directly to the youth. It couldn't be used to hire mentors.

An outside agency offered to fund one mentor for a year and to observe progress. We wanted to hire someone who was a former foster youth, but we couldn't find one who had their life together enough to successfully do the job. At that time, I was working as a telemarketer. Although I was making good money I hated my job. So I decided to apply for the position and got it.

Mentor Match

Many youths leaving foster care didn't have basic identification such as birth certificates, government identification and social security cards. Potential employers couldn't hire those youth since they weren't able to provide them with those documents.

Those youth were assigned to me. My job included helping them apply for those documents, locate housing, find a job, and enroll in school. I had twenty youth on my caseload at one at a time. At the end of the year, the results were outstanding. Almost all the youth I had helped were working, going to school and had stable living arrangements. I shared the results with the funder who was blown away and offered to fund the position for another four years.

The Mentor Match program was so successful, it became a national model. I began training other organizations across the nation on how to mentor and support former foster youth. Newspapers, magazines, and television shows interviewed me on a regular basis. I was also invited to testify before the United States Congress.

I also helped develop and Independent Living Program for foster and homeless teens. We purchased several apartments and a large facility for the youth to engage in activities and classes. We helped over 3,000 youths per year. For the first time in my life, I woke up every day feeling thrilled to go to work. Five years later I resigned to attend college with my brother.

Community College

While at dinner one evening, Brad asked me if I made plans for college. I told him I hadn't made a plan but that I always liked the thought of having an MBA. After a bit more conversation, Brad offered to pay for my tuition and the textbooks for my first college class.

The next day, I stopped by the local community college and picked up a class catalog. I looked through it to see if any of the classes were of interest to me. One class jumped out at me, a photograph-developing class. I was involved in photography both personally and professionally at that time. I worked as a photographer for a tour company and I enjoyed taking pictures in my free time. So I thought taking that class would be useful to me in both areas. When I called Brad, he gave me the money, and I enrolled.

I showed up very excited to the first day of class. Then I found out the professor would be showing us basic photography tips as well. I became super excited at that point. Our homework included taking specific types of photos such as side profiles, action, and close-up shots.

A month later, I began worrying since I didn't have the time or desire to take the photos as the professor instructed. We needed them for the photo development portion of the class and the final grade. Then I remembered I was only taking the class for fun.

On the last day before the photos were needed, I took a bunch of random photos so I could participate in the development portion of the class. As we were developing the photos, the professor saw that my photos had nothing to do with the ones he recommended.

He asked me if I understood the assignment. When I said that I did, he then asked me why I chose to take those photos instead. I told him that I took those photos yesterday so I would have something to develop in class that day. I also told him that I didn't care about the grade since I was taking the class for fun. He looked at me stunned for a few seconds. Then smiled and said, "Fair enough," and walked away.

I attended the class a few more times and quit once the development portion was over. Brad wasn't thrilled about it, he thought I should have at least finished the class.

The next semester, Brad offered to pay for a class again as long as I finished it. If I passed it, he would pay for the next one as well. I agreed to his terms and took Sociology 101. I really liked the class, the professor was a bit of a nut, which made it fun. I liked a few girls in the class as well. But I was too scared to say anything other than hello or goodbye.

I read the textbook and did the homework when I could and I got a B in the class. Brad said he was proud of me and offered to pay for two classes next time. If I took just two classes a semester, I could have a Bachelor's degree in ten years. At first, it seemed like a lot of time, but then I realized that ten years was going by one way or another. I would either have the degree or I wouldn't.

The next semester, I took Communications 101 and Political Science 101. During the Political Science class, the professor said he was arranging a trip to Washington D.C. for the semester break and any student who passed the class and could afford it, was welcome to come.

The trip was awesome and the professor was an amazing tour guide. We toured museums, monuments, the Capitol Building, the White House and sat in on a case being argued at the Supreme Court.

I continued to take two classes a semester until it it became a burden. Then I transferred my credits to an Online University so I could earn my degree faster. Five years later, I received a Bachelor's Degree in Marketing.

Reconnecting With Turtle

I reconnected with my brother, Turtle when I was twenty-one years old. We met up once and he never returned my messages afterwards. Although I was really sad, I still followed him on social media.

One evening, my boss and I went to the bar next door for dinner and to plan an upcoming fundraising event. As we were leaving, a man at the bar caught my attention. He had a tattoo on his arm that was similar to my brother's tattoo. An overwhelming feeling rushed through my body that the man at the bar was my brother. However, I just ignored the feeling and walked out of the bar.

As we stepped outside, I told my boss that I thought my brother was sitting at the bar. She was a bit shocked and asked why I thought so. I told her the tattoo seemed familiar for some reason as if I had seen it before. She suggested I go back and ask him if he was my brother. I was so scared that I told her it probably wasn't my brother as I started walking back to the office.

As I took two steps away from the bar, I felt a sense of regret rushing through me. I stopped and told my boss that I was going to find out. I walked back inside the bar, tapped the man on the shoulder and asked him if his name was Turtle. When he said it was his name, he seemed to be confused. Then I asked him if his last name was Walley. When he said yes again, I got very excited. When I told him my name was Chris, he just said, "Hi," and turned around to continue watching the football game.

I was a bit shocked. For some reason, I expected him to know who I was and to be thrilled to see me again as much as I was in seeing him. Then I said, "It's Chris, your brother," and asked if I could sit and watch the game with him. When he said that I could, I took a seat.

At first, the conversation was a bit awkward, but eventually, it smoothed out and we wound up hanging out for the rest of the night.

College With Turtle

One day, Turtle and I were looking at college websites together. I was thinking about obtaining a Masters Degree, while he desired to finish up his Bachelor's Degree. We found a school we both liked. They only served organic, vegetarian food in the dining hall. The students and professors meditated before and after class. And the school was a leader in the field of Sustainability.

A few weeks later, Turtle told me he wanted to attend when the next semester started in a few months. I told him it was a great idea but that I still had a year to go before I could attend. When he asked me if there was anything I could do to speed it up, I told him that I would try by calling my college counselor to see if there was anything I could do.

Later that week, my counselor and I chatted on the phone. When I told him about what I wanted to achieve, he told me that there was a way to do it by using a tool called "credit by exam." Essentially, if I took a course's final test and passed, I would get credit for the course. The course fees were $80 while the courses the school offered were about $500 each. He said that I could take up to seven classes that way. After we hung up, I spent the rest of the day researching that option.

I was already in college full-time and would need to pass a test once every two weeks. But if I did that, I could finish a year of college classes in three months. Then I could head off to school with my brother and rebuild our relationship. I took Turtle out to lunch the next day and shared what I had learned. He was excited and encouraged me to pursue it, which I did.

I studied for almost fifteen hours each day and at the end of three months, I received my degree. A few weeks later, we packed up our things and headed off to college together.

In the beginning, it was a bit awkward and we struggle to connect. But eventually, we figured things out and had a blast together. A year later, I graduated with a

Master's Degree and we parted ways. We still communicate on a regular basis.

Finding My Family

When I was twenty years old, my girlfriend asked me if I would be interested in finding my parents. I told her I was interested in finding my dad, but not my mom. I was still upset at her.

She took it upon herself to lead the effort and paid an organization to conduct an online search. She provided them with my dad's name, social security number, and any other relevant information I had about him. I wasn't aware that she was doing that, but when she told me I was both thrilled and extremely nervous. What if he was a terrible person, or worse, wanted nothing to do with me.

The organization conducted a search and provided my girlfriend with three addresses in California where he might be living. I wrote a letter and sent it off to the three addresses. A few weeks later, my girlfriend showed up at my work to tell me that my dad's wife had called her.

Later that night, I spoke with my dad on the phone for the first time in my life. I don't recall what we talked about but I remember being filled with both joy and anxiety.

A month later, we took a trip to Los Angeles to meet him. Our visit just happened to fall on Father's Day that year. I was nervous during the entire ride to Los Angeles.

The night we arrived, I pulled him aside and asked him to share his side of the story. He started by telling me that he had tried to get custody of me but that he couldn't afford the legal fees. He also said that, on my eighteenth birthday, he called the state to see if I needed help with college. The state official told him they had no idea who I was or who he was. He thought I was living with my mother the entire time.

The next day, we went to dinner with my grandmother, aunts, and cousins. It was a bit weird to interact with these people at first. They were familiar with me but I wasn't familiar with them. I was so happy having my girlfriend to turn to when things got a bit uncomfortable.

When we headed back to Las Vegas, I felt so excited to finally have a family of my own!

After I received my Master's Degree, I decided to spend the next few years building relationships with the rest of my family. I moved out to Los Angeles, California for a few years to build relationships with my aunts and cousins. There was some head-butting at times, but it felt amazing to finally have a family of my own.

And after that, I moved to Arizona (where I currently reside) to build a relationship with my dad, stepmom, and siblings. It feels fantastic to spend birthdays and holidays with family now.

Chapter 27
Next Steps

Now that I've gone to college, found my family, finished this book, and healed my spirit it's time for me to get back to work! Over the next few years, I'll be traveling around the country connecting with and counseling foster youth. Helping them to understand why foster care happens and what they can learn from it. I would love to meet you in person someday.

To hear your thoughts and feelings about the book, foster care, or life in general. Please stop by and say hi if I'm ever in a town near you.

To learn more visit:

www.40Parents.com/NextSteps